The Eclectus Parrot:

The Complete Guide to Subspecies, Breeding, Diet, Selling, Owning and Mating.

By Graham Taylor

Acknowledgements

Writing a book such as this an author seeks advice and assistance from many people, from all walks of life. I would like to acknowledge and thank all those friends who have given me that assistance. My wife Marcia and my daughter Lisa who gave me their encouragement to complete the manuscript and special thanks to my son David who without his skills with the computer there may not have been a book at all.

My thanks to Laurella Desborough of the United States for her insight into the keeping and breeding of Eclectus parrots in that country and for providing a chapter titled " Companion Eclectus in the United States of America" for this book. To my other friends Oskar Kirsche, Graham Bradley, Rosemary Low, Ray Ackroyd, Don Wells, Mr.Swoboda and Dr.Bagus Nugraha of Bali Bird Park, Indonesia, Frank Lambert senior conservation advisor, Indonesia for BirdLife International, Carole McCormick of Birdlife International, United Kingdom.

A special thanks to Martina Mueller curator of birds at Walsrode Vogelpark Germany for her assistance on the two rare sub species *Eclectus roratus cornelia* and *Eclectus roratus riedeli.*

I would also like to thank a small group of men, who without their courage and skills a lot of the information contained in this book would not have been possible. These men would risk their lives numerous times a day scaling the trees of the rainforest. They are simply known as "climbers".

Graham Taylor
graham@eclectus-parrots.com

Contents

Introduction

The Eclectus parrot. So distinctively different, where the male is a deep forest green and the female brilliant red with deep cobalt blue breast. These unique parrots were thought to be of two separate species when first discovered during the 1700s, today the Eclectus parrot can be seen in many zoological and breeding collections around the world.

My involvement with these magnificent birds was by accident: the year was 1967; I was living in Sydney, Australia. At that time I was a specialist breeder of black cockatoos, the only black cockatoo I had not kept or bred at that time was the great Palm Cockatoo *Probosciger aterrimus*. Little was known about their avicultural requirements in captivity, in fact at that time they had never been photographed in the wild.

Over the next few months I planned a bird watching trip to Cape York Peninsula, far north Queensland to study these birds in their wild state. My trip received some publicity in the local press and drew the attention of an American film producer who was visiting Australia scouting for suitable locations to produce a documentary. He gave me a call and came out to meet me the following weekend. After many meetings the size of the group grew from three, my wife Marcia and I and our two and a half year old daughter Lisa, to a party of nine; two Americans, one German and six Australians.

In July 1968 we left Sydney in a convoy of five four-wheel drive Land Rovers for Iron Range, Cape York Peninsula. During the eight weeks we spent at Iron Range filming the Palm cockatoos, I began to watch these beautiful bright red and almost iridescent green parrots sometimes in pairs but mostly in small groups of eight to ten birds. These birds of course were Eclectus Parrots, *Eclectus roratus macgillivrayi,* the Australian sub species.

I was so fascinated by these birds that on our return to Sydney I phoned around the bird dealers to see if I could obtain a pair of these Australian sub species. But only the Red Sided Eclectus, *Eclectus roratus polychloros* or New Guinea Eclectus, were available. I purchased a pair and thus began a thirty-two-year association with Eclectus parrots.

Four years later my wife, daughter and I packed up all our belongings and moved 1800 miles north to Cairns, north Queensland, to live and to develop a bird park to house and display Australian parrots and cockatoos.

In 1973 after the development of the bird park had been completed and we had opened to the public I applied for a collecting permit to collect Palm cockatoos and Eclectus parrots as well as some other species found in Cape York. These birds would be for educational display and captive breeding programs; I had to wait a further two years before the permit was issued. I made plans to return to Iron Range during the coming breeding seasons to study these birds.

There is a full chapter on collecting of Eclectus parrots included in this book as very few aviculturists have the chance or the time to spend in the rainforest to study these majestic birds. Reading this chapter alone I hope will help all Eclectus breeders to understand a little of the way we should feed, house and breed these birds.

From my Cape York diaries covering over a dozen expeditions to the rainforest of far north Queensland from a period from 1968 to 1985, enjoy with me as I relive the trials and tribulations of dusty roads, flooded rivers, cyclones and torrential rain not to mention taipan snakes and crocodiles.

One problem that faces us all as breeders of these birds is identification. This book and the photographs contained within will assist in this task, each sub species being shown in a series of photographs. Each sub species will be described in a way that will not confuse you. As a breeder I find it frustrating when I purchase a new bird book to identify a particular sub species. I often find it hard to understand the text and by the time I am finished I am more confused than ever. I hope you find the descriptions in this book easy to understand.

A chapter on companion Eclectus parrots in the United States of America by noted breeder and author Laurella Desborough will give an insight into the keeping of Eclectus parrots as pets.

Up to date information gathered over the last three years from the latest field reports has been included for each sub species, area maps showing locations where each sub species are found are also included.

Information on the rarer sub species *Eclectus roratus riedeli* and *Eclectus roratus cornelia* are included. These two sub species, in particular *Eclectus roratus riedeli,* have just recently come into captivity in Europe so all known sub species are now breeding in captivity.

I do hope you find this book on the Eclectus parrot as interesting as I have in writing it. These fascinating birds that have been part of my life now for the past thirty-two years will always be very special to me. Enjoy this book.

Graham Taylor.

Chapter 1
Genus Eclectus

The Eclectus genus consists of one nominate and eight sub species depending on which reference guide you care to follow. In Forshaw's *parrots of the world* 1973 edition he cites ten sub species including *Eclectus roratus westermani.* This sub species is only known from a few aviary specimens of more than a hundred years or so ago and is now described as *Eclectus roratus roratus,* although there is still some doubt due to its size of 33cm.

In his book *The Eclectus a complete guide* by Roger Sweeney, 1993 edition, he states that there are seven sub species. He chooses to leave out the sub species *Eclectus roratus biaki* and *Eclectus roratus aruensis* because there is still some dispute over their validity.

As an aviculturalist, who has specialized in Eclectus parrots for quite a number of years, I believe that the two sub species *Eclectus roratus biaki* and *Eclectus roratus aruensis* should be regarded as distinct sub species. A number of breeding pairs of both these sub species are held in collections in the United States, Germany, Spain, and probably in the U.K. as well. The argument is that these sub species are found on islands close to the New Guinea / West Papua mainland and overlap areas where *Eclectus roratus polychloros* are found and therefore should be called *Eclectus roratus polychloros.* In my view this does not hold up: you only have to see these birds in captivity alongside the other more recognizable sub species to realize there something different about them.

If we take the argument further and we look at the Australian sub species, *Eclectus roratus macgillivrayi,* which is found on the eastern side of Cape York Peninsula northern Australia. This, the largest of the sub species is located only 256 km (160 m) from the tip of Cape York and is not found on any of the islands of the Torres Strait. These islands that I sailed through in 1974, you are never out of the sight of land and many migratory birds travel these straits north and south each year but no Eclectus parrots have been recorded making this trip.

While collecting in the Cape York area in the 1970s it was amazing to me each time I went there that you are driving through dry and dusty bush tracks on one side of the Tozer Range. This is part of the Great Dividing Range that runs along the entire East Coast of Australia. You see birds of the open forest woodland. And once you pass through Tozer's Gap heading due east for the coast there is a dramatic change you are no longer traveling on dusty tracks or open forest—, its now deep thick green jungle with many running creeks and rivers. There is a coolness in the air, there is a major difference which is not apparent at first, but once you have gathered your thoughts you realize that all the bird calls are different. You are now hearing the birds of the rainforest.

In this area of Iron Range there are twenty-eight bird species that are not found in any other part of Australia. These unique birds including the Eclectus parrot *Eclectus roratus macgillivrayi* are only found here in this somewhat small rainforest pocket bounded by the Rocky River to the south and the Pascoe River to the north, south west to the Peach River district of Blue Mountain and due west to Mount Tozer.

The Eclectus parrots are great flyers and are often seen flying high above the canopy of the rainforest. But in my experience and the time that I have spent in the rainforest observing them, to me they are localized and do not travel great distances except to feed and roost. But only in their locality. As breeders of these birds we all know what good breeders they are in captivity, in the wild if the season is right breeding pairs will produce more than one clutch. Feeding these fledglings takes time and what they feed on is found in the rainforest. Although Eclectus parrots can be seen in the open forest (in fact sometimes they nest in the open forest), they have to return to the rainforest to feed.

My argument for the individual status of *Eclectus roratus biaki* and *Eclectus roratus aruensis* is the same as my reasons for the Australian sub species *Eclectus roratus macgillivrayi*— they are a localized sub species.

Eclectus Parrot sub species.

1. The Grand Eclectus, *Eclectus roratus roratus.*

The Grand Eclectus *Eclectus roratus roratus* is regarded as the nominate race. The male of this sub species was first described in the 1700s and it was a further hundred years before the female was described.

The Eclectus parrot is unique as it's the only member of the parrot family where the female is brighter and better looking than the male, her bright red appearance with a contrasting purple nape and breast making a striking sight when you see these birds for the first time.

The Grand Eclectus *Eclectus roratus roratus* are found in Indonesia, on the islands of the central and southern Maluku, including Ambon, Buru, and Seram. They are also found on two smaller islands to the north east of Ambon, Haruka and Saparua in the Lease Group. The Grand Eclectus that occur on Seram are smaller in size compared to the birds that are found on Ambon. Males from both locations are similar and only vary in size, where females differ in their feather coloration to their breast and under-tail coverts. Females found on Seram have a blending of the red and lavender breast feathers (similar to the Vosmaeri subspecies) these females also have more yellowish under-tail feathers. Females found on Ambon are larger and have a distinct separation of the red and lavender breast feathers, forming a bib.

For hundreds of years these birds as well as many other species of parrots, lories and cockatoos have been traded between islands of the Indonesian archipelago. The Grand Eclectus was one of the most often offered species and many thousands of birds were shipped through the central port of Ambon.

During the 1960s and 70s Eclectus were shipped in large numbers from Ambon to the major bird exporters in Jakarta and then onto Europe, and the United States. The Vosmaeri Eclectus *Eclectus roratus vosmaeri* would be the most widely kept sub species in these countries, only limited numbers of Grand Eclectus *Eclectus roratus roratus* are found in the United States.

Although Eclectus are protected throughout Indonesia and cannot be exported, it is not illegal to own or trade them domestically. If ever you have the chance to visit the port city of Ambon, spend some time at the ferry terminal watching the passengers arriving from the other parts of the Malukus (Moluccas). There you will see many birds and animals in bamboo cages, as part of their luggage. These weekly visitors come to Ambon on market day, where these birds and animals including Eclectus parrots are sold or traded. Some do reach other countries. I have heard of a collector in Thailand who owns a fleet of fishing boats that do regular trips throughout these Indonesian islands and returns with birds as part of his cargo of fish.

Lambert (1993) reports that there is a great deal of evidence to suggest that much of the trade in parrots from the Malukus is being conducted involving Butonese traders operating from Tukangbesi islands in south Sulawesi to Singapore.

Eclectus parrots, although protected from trapping and trade by Indonesian law, are still caught in small numbers in the Malukus. Lambert states that this level of trapping is not believed to be significant.

The Grand Eclectus *Eclectus roratus roratus* status in the wild seems fairly secure: Trapping numbers of *Eclectus roratus roratus* at present are relatively small and Lambert reports that this is less than 5 percent of the total catch of parrots from Maluku. The number of *Eclectus roratus roratus* trapped by villagers each year is between 375and 480 birds.

This subspecies has declined further throughout its full range since the 1950s, due to trapping. Bowler and Taylor 1989 state that on Seram, Eclectus are fairly common in all wooded habitats from the coastal mangroves to about 800m. A pair was seen at nest near Solea during late August and early September.

2. Vosmaeri Eclectus, *Eclectus roratus vosmaeri.*

The Vosmaeri or Vosmaer's Eclectus *Eclectus roratus vosmaeri* is found on the islands of Halmahera, Obi, Bacan and Sula in the northern Malukus. This sub species is the most northerly found member of the Eclectus genus. Slightly larger than the Grand Eclectus, this sub species was trapped and exported in very large numbers during the 1960s and 70s and would be the most commonly kept of the nine sub species in aviculture.

On Halmahera and Bacan Islands they are regarded as common. On Obi Island they are rare, being recorded only a few times near Kelo. Once common on Obi Island they declined during the 1950s where agricultural crops were protected from the feeding parrots.

The female Vosmaeri Eclectus would have to be one of the most strikingly beautiful parrots I have ever seen. And yet I have not seen a photograph that does justice to this bird's beauty. Her overall red appearance, paler than the other members of this species, the blending of her breast from pale red to lavender and with no defined bib, the yellow under tail coverts, red tail feathers and bright buttercup yellow band to the tip, makes this bird somewhat unmistakable.

When visiting Indonesia in 1973 and again in 1974 the Vosmaeri Eclectus was a common sight at bird markets in Jakarta. At that time Eclectus parrots were not protected as they are now and could be purchased for a few dollars. It was during this period that thousands of bird species were exported from the main export center of Jakarta. A great number of these species were lories, cockatoos and parrots including most of the Eclectus sub species, except for the two rarer sub species *Eclectus roratus cornelia* and *Eclectus roratus riedeli* from Sumba and Tanimbar islands.

During this trip to Indonesia in 1973 I decided to visit the bird market at Pasar Burung, I was told that this market was the largest in Indonesia and many bird species that I had never seen before would be there. A group of us from the hotel boarded a mini bus for our short trip across the city to Pasar Burung. On this bus I met a German bird importer who was visiting Jakarta to arrange a shipment of parrots, cockatoos and lories to export back to Germany. He spoke very good English and as I did not speak German, we became friends.

On arrival at the bird market we walked around with our Indonesian guide to look at the birds. It was amazing— thousands of birds from small finches to eagles and owls, but it was the parrots and cockatoos we wanted to see, my interest in birds at the time was cockatoos, black cockatoos in particular.

I did not expect to see any here. But there just ahead of us was a cage of five Palm cockatoos. I asked our guide to ask where they came from. We were told they came from Merauke, Irian Jaya, and West Papua. I then asked the price and was told US$ 300 each. Our guide then told us it would be much cheaper if he purchased it for us. As we were only looking at the time we moved on.

It was here at Pasar Burung that I saw Vosmaeri Eclectus for the first time. At this market as well as many of the bird markets throughout Indonesia, many of the parrots, cockatoos and lories were tame and were sold to you sitting on a perch with a leg tied by a short lead to this perch. This way they attract a much higher price as many of these birds are sold locally as pets. There were many Eclectus, both tame and in wooden cages. The Vosmaeri female was so striking to me, maybe because I had not seen them before except in bird books. They were not yet available in Australia, and did not become available until around 1992.

That night my wife and I had dinner with the German importer and we talked about the birds we saw that day. He could see that I was fascinated by the Vosmaeri Eclectus. He asked if I would like to join him the next day when he was to meet one of Indonesia's largest exporters of birds. Without hesitation I agreed.

Early the next morning we were picked up by the exporter's driver and driven to his bird farm a short distance out of the city. Here the exporter greeted us. We were invited in and offered tea and a short time later we were shown around his bird farm. There were a number of large sheds or warehouse type buildings; inside were rows of suspended cages containing every bird you ever wanted to see. There were species I did not even know, let alone seen before.

Some of the species we saw were soft bills, doves, pigeons, finches and even bird of paradise from West Papua, shinning starlings and hornbills were available as well.

The parrots, cockatoos, and lories were in large numbers, sometimes 50 to a 100 in each cage. Just some of the species we saw were Ambonian King Parrot *Alisterus amboinensis,* Green Winged King Parrot *Alisterus chloropterus,* Great Billed Parrot *Tanygnathus megalorynchos*, and five species of fig parrots, Salvadori's Fig Parrot *Psittaculirostris salvadorii,* Edwards Fig Parrot *Psittaculirostris edwardsii,* Desmarests Fig Parrot *Psittaculirostris desmarestii*, Double Eyed Fig Parrot *Opopsitta diophthalma*, and the Orange Breasted Fig Parrot *Opopsitta gulielmiterti.*

Cockatoo's species seen were Goffins Cockatoo *Cacatua goffini,* White Cockatoo *Cacatua alba,* the Lesser Sulphur Crested Cockatoo *Cacatua sulphurea,* and the now endangered Salmon Crested Cockatoo *Cacatua moluccensis.* There were also twenty or so Palm Cockatoos *Probosciger aterrimus* of the sub species *stenolophus.*

There were a large number of lories, far to many to mention here but to name just a few that may be of interest: Black Capped Lory *Lorius lory,* and Rainbow Lory *Tricoglossus haematodus*, Dusky Lory *Pseudeos fuscata,* Red Lory *Eos bornea,* Red and Blue Lory *Eos histrio,* Duyvenbode's Lory *Chalcopsitta duivenbodei,* Black Lory *Chalcopsitta atra,* and there were many Chattering Lories *Lorius garrulus.*

And we saw many Eclectus parrots that day, mostly Grand Eclectus *Eclectus roratus roratus* and Vosmaeri Eclectus *Eclectus roratus vosmaeri.* While I was waiting for my German friend to conclude his business a large shipment of birds had just arrived by truck from the airport. I was very interested in watching the unloading of these crates of birds. There were many crates containing Eclectus parrots. I asked one of the Indonesian workers where they came from, and he said Ambon.

When the workers opened the crates and released the birds into a larger holding aviary, I saw the best pairs of Vosmaeri Eclectus ever. I know I saw them for the first time the day before at Pasar Burung bird market but these were absolutely beautiful, the males were bright forest green with a tinge of yellow through it, their long slender bodies, their feathers seemed to glisten in the sun.

The females were equally as nice as the males with their beautiful lavender breast and buttercup yellow tails.

Later when I returned to the others I had to ask the price of these great looking Vosmaeri Eclectus, although I knew I could not take them back with me to Australia, due to our customs and quarantine laws. Little did I know then it would be another twenty-three years before I would purchase my first pair of these fascinating birds. The price of the pair of Vosmaeri in 1973 was U.S. $70.

3. Tanimbar Eclectus, *Eclectus roratus riedeli.*

The Tanimbar Eclectus as the name suggests are found in the Tanimbar Islands in the Banda Sea, Indonesia. Also known as Riedel's Eclectus or Riedeli Eclectus parrot, this rare sub species was named by Meyer in 1881 after Dr. Riedel, a resident of Ambon. This is the second smallest sub species of Eclectus parrot and is quite unique.

Like Cornelia's Eclectus, *Eclectus roratus cornelia,* the female of this sub species is entirely red. It differs from Cornelia by having yellow under tail coverts and a much broader buttercup yellow tip of the tail. The overall red appearance of this bird is darker than Cornelia.

The male Riedeli Eclectus parrot is, out of the nine sub species of male Eclectus, the only one that is easily identifiable. The majority of breeders of Eclectus parrots have great difficulty in separating the males into sub species. Because they are basically green birds with red under the wings and varying amounts of pale yellow to their tail tips, identification becomes difficult.

The male Riedeli Eclectus is the only sub species that has a broad buttercup yellow band to both sides of the tail. This band is somewhat larger than the band of yellow that is found on the female Vosmaeri Eclectus parrot, *Eclectus roratus vosmaeri.*

The Tanimbar Eclectus parrot was practically unknown to aviculture until 1995, when Walsrode Bird Park in Germany received some birds from Indonesia.

Martina Mueller, the Curator of birds there, told me that from 1995 to 1997 they received the sub species *Eclectus roratus cornelia, Eclectus roratus riedeli* and *Eclectus roratus aruensis* and had success in breeding them shortly after. To date they have bred 0.1 *Eclectus roratus aruensis* in 1996, 0.2 *Eclectus roratus cornelia* in 1997 and 2.0 *Eclectus roratus riedeli* in 99/00. They also breed *Eclectus roratus vosmaeri* on a regular basis.

The successful breeding of these two rare sub species *Eclectus roratus cornelia* and *Eclectus roratus riedeli* is very good news for the future survival of these sub species. With species management and breeding programs in place it should not be to long before these rare sub species become readily available to aviculture.

The status in the wild of the Tanimbar Eclectus is largely unknown. Field

Reports dating back to 1985 have little to say about this sub species. Verbelen, 1994, reports that Riedeli is uncommon on Yamdena, the main island of Tanimbar. Logging is carried out on these islands by large companies and the pace of deforestation is at an alarming rate. Verbelen also reports that the "political situation" between the local people and the logging companies has resulted in heavy fighting taking place. Tourists are discouraged to go there during these periods.

4. Cornelia Eclectus, *Eclectus roratus cornelia.*

Confined to the island of Sumba, Indonesia, the Cornelia's Eclectus *Eclectus roratus cornelia* is larger than the nominate race. The female of this sub species, although similar to the female Riedeli Eclectus parrot being entirely red in appearance, lacks the yellow under tail coverts and the buttercup yellow tail band. The overall red appearance is brighter than the female Riedeli Eclectus.

The male Cornelia is similar to the Grand Eclectus but larger, the head and nape area appears a lighter green, and its tail feathers have more blue suffused with the green.

Sumba Island lies south east of the Indonesian tourist island of Bali, formerly the Lesser Sunda Islands now called Nusa Tenggara, which means 'South East Islands'. This sub species is the second rarest of the Eclectus parrot sub species. Only limited numbers of *Eclectus roratus cornelia* are in captivity and the latest field reports state that their numbers in the wild are vulnerable. Marsden & Jones 1989 reports that a survey conducted on Sumba estimated the population of Cornelia

Eclectus at around 34,900 birds. Marsden & Jones 1997 survey of nesting requirements for parrots on Sumba states that a total of 132 nests of Sumba's parrots and endemic species of hornbill were located. Nearly half were in trees, containing other parrot or hornbill nests; one tree contained five active nests. Most of these trees were at a height of 38m (125ft).

Deciduous trees of the *Datiscaceae* family were most often preferred with 8 percent of nests of *Geoffroyus geoffroyi* and 83 percent for *Eclectus roratus cornelia.*

Sumba has five parrot and one hornbill species. The parrot species are Citron Crested Cockatoo *Cacatua sulphurea citrinocristata,* Great Billed Parrot *Tanygnathus megalorynchos sumbensis,* the Rainbow Lorikeet *Trichoglossus haematodus,* the Red Cheeked Parrot *Geoffroyus geoffroyi,* and the Eclectus Parrot *Eclectus roratus cornelia.* The single Hornbill species is *Rhyticeros everetti.* Marsden, Jones and Linsley 1989 and 1992 also states that 21 birds, mostly female, were seen in captivity at Waingapu and Melolo, east Sumba, and this continued trade should, if possible, be curtailed. Although the estimate of 34,900 may be lower than the actual size, this sub species is at great risk of extinction. Category of threat: Endangered.

With an estimate of 34,900 birds, it may not be too late to save this sub species of Eclectus parrot. And with the present illegal trade of these birds from Sumba through Ambon to Jakarta in recent years, the actual numbers may be considerably less. One would hope that the limited numbers now breeding in captivity will have enough genetic diversity to allow this beautiful and unique sub species to survive.

The four sub species of *Eclectus roratus* listed above are a group of birds where the females of all the four sub species lack the blue orbital eye ring.

In the following five sub species, all females have the blue orbital eye ring.

5. Aru Island Eclectus, *Eclectus roratus aruensis*.

The Aru Island Eclectus *Eclectus roratus aruensis* is confined as its name suggests to the Aru Islands of Indonesia. This group of islands is the most eastern islands of Maluku, and lies about 100 miles south of the West Papua mainland in the Arafura Sea.

Mostly consisting of low swampy islands the Arus cover a total area of 3,306 square miles (8,563 square km) there are six main islands: Warilau, Kola, Wokam, Koboor, Maikoor and Trangan. About eighty five smaller islands are separated by five narrow channels. Dobo, the capital, on the small island of Wamer has the main seaport and airport. These islands are covered with dense forest and coastal swamps, the wildlife is Papuan with a strong Australian affinity, and marsupials are the dominant mammals.

Aru Island Eclectus parrots are larger than the nominate race, both male and female are slender in appearance, have longer tails than the Red Sided Eclectus *Eclectus roratus polychloros*. The male is a darker emerald green with a tinge of blue suffused throughout the head, nape down to the mantle; the tail is tipped with pale lemon. The eye is reddish/orange.

The female is similar to *Eclectus roratus polychloros* but larger overall and has a longer tail; the head is a brighter red than *Eclectus roratus polychloros*. The blue bib is somewhat smaller than the Red Sided; the eye is creamy white.

With reasonable numbers of the Aru Island Eclectus in captivity in Spain, Germany and the United States and with captive breeding and species management programs in place this sub species appears secure. There are few field reports coming out of the Arus because of its isolation from the rest of Indonesia. Very few visitors go there, because of the lack of regular flights to and from these islands. The wild population of *Eclectus roratus aruensis* seems to be reasonably secure.

I had, along with two of my friends, sailed through these islands in 1974. We were on our way back from Ambon, the main port of the Malukus. After spending two weeks cruising Cream, Buru and Ambon, we were heading home to Australia. We arrived at the southern tip of Aru late one evening and decided to refuel the diesel tanks from 44gal.drums we had stowed in the front hold. We could see lights from the village on the island. It was the month of July but because we were close to the equator it was very hot and humid. After we had emptied three or four drums of diesel into the main tanks, we decided to anchor there for the night. We pushed the empty drums over the side and they floated towards the shore.

Because the nights were so hot we mostly slept up on deck, as we did this night. Next morning just after dawn I was awaken by sounds of strange voices and splashing of water. As I started to sit up and peer over the side rail, I could not believe my eyes. Here was about 15 or 20 dugout canoes, each with two or three natives heading towards us. I woke the others not knowing what we were in for. The three of us stood there gazing towards these natives, still not quite awake. We thought of what we could do, was it to be a hostile meeting!

We knew we did not have enough time to raise the anchor and just sail away, so we decided to see if we talk to them and see what they wanted. I had a lot of experience with the Aborigines in Cape York Peninsula, northern Australia, who I found to be very friendly. I said to the others lets see if any of them are smiling, my two mates Kevin and Gary both looked at me as if to say "you have got to be crazy"— you want us to see if their smiling. We looked at this group of people franticly paddling towards us to see if any of them had a smile on their face, and sure enough there in one of the leading canoes was this huge man with the biggest grin on his face waving to us.

I gestured to my two mates that all was okay, and told them to smile and wave. They came alongside and I offered my hand to the man with the large grin, he accepted and I beckoned him aboard. He could not speak a word of English or Indonesian for that matter; it was some sort of local dialect. He then pointed to another man sitting in the canoe and waved him to come aboard. He spoke a little broken English. We then found out what all the fuss was about. It turned out to be about the 44gal.drums we dropped over the side the night before. These drums floated ashore and were quickly retrieved by the locals. Apparently these drums are highly valued by them as they are used to make stoves and other items around the village.

What has this got to do with Eclectus parrots, you might ask? Well, that turned out to be interesting. With broken English and sign language they wanted us to go ashore with them. Not sure what to do we had a brief discussion about it, our main concern was our boat. If we all went ashore who would watch the boat. We had heard stories about villagers stealing from ships that stopped at these out of the way islands throughout Indonesia, and we were worried about it.

It was agreed that we could see the boat from the village and we would all keep an eye on it. The three of us boarded their canoes and they took us ashore, upon landing we were surrounded by dozens of screaming children and village women. The man with the big grin who we nicknamed "smiley" came up to us along with the one who spoke a little English, he asked which one of us was the captain. Not knowing what this was all about Gary and I quickly pointed to Kevin and said he was the skipper.

In fact Kevin was the skipper and a great one at that, but just to be safe Gary and I, not knowing what they had instore for us did not hesitate in pointing to Kevin.

About four huge men picked up Kevin and sat him on their shoulders and started walking into the center of the village. There was this rather large grass thatched hut, sitting on timber posts, Kevin was taken inside, we were made to stay outside, we waited for about half an hour and then Kevin appeared. He was smiling, thank God for that!

Kevin said they just offered him food and some kind of drink, which tasted like tree bark, and left him a little light headed. They had asked him for more fuel drums and anything else we would like to trade. We decided to give them as many drums as we could before we left the next day, they offered us food and drink and we stayed quite a few hours.

It was very hot and Kevin was starting to feel the effects of the drink he had had earlier. He wanted to return to our boat. We started to say our good-byes and began walking through the village when I heard an Eclectus parrot call. I pointed to where I thought I heard the calling come from, and started to walk in that direction. There under one of the huts were a few rough timber cages of birds. In one of these cages there were five Aru Island Eclectus parrots, three females and two males; the other birds were White Cockatoo *Cacatua galerita eleonora,* and some Red Flanked Lorikeets *Charmosyna placentis.*

I asked Smiley what they were for and he said to trade to the bird dealers that call to these islands about once every two months. He said they catch as many birds as they can to supplement the village income, I was curious to know what price he would be paid for these birds. So I asked how much did he get for them. It worked out that he only received about two U.S. dollars for the Lorikeets and Eclectus and eight dollars for the Cockatoos.

It's amazing to me that the people that need the money the most benefit the least, when you consider the price we as aviculturists pay for these birds at the retail end of the market.

Kevin, Gary and I were returned to our boat safe and well, except for Kevin who had a huge headache and went below to lie down. Gary and I emptied another five fuel drums into the main tanks and gave them to the villagers. We said our good-byes and they paddled towards the shore. Early the next morning we set sail for home.

Eclectus parrots have been traded for many hundreds of years throughout these islands of Indonesia, in the latest field reports that I have received this is still the case. I might add that although Eclectus parrots are protected in Indonesia and cannot be exported, it is not illegal to own or trade them domestically. Birds do reach other countries; the trading of wildlife in Indonesia is in fact a way of life. Corruption and bribery is also the way many of these protected species reach outside countries.

During our sailing trip to the island of Ambon in 1974, we were offered birds from dugout canoes within minutes of docking at port Ambon. This harbour, next to Sydney harbour, would have to be one of the nicest I have seen, deep dark blue and when the tide was in crystal clear. Ambon harbour was a very large harbour and many naval ships were there. Not far from us were ships of the Indonesian navy. After we cleared customs and immigration we were invited to one of these ships. Not long after we boarded we noticed quite a few bamboo cages of birds on the after deck. When I asked what they were, I was told that they were pets owned by the crew and were purchased while on duty throughout the outer islands of Indonesia.

There were Eclectus Parrots *Eclectus roratus roratus* and *Eclectus roratus vosmaeri,* Great Bill Parrots *Tanygnathus megalorynchos* and some Racket-tail Parrots *Prioniturus platurus* as well as White Cockatoos *Cacatua alba* and Lesser Sulphur-Crested Cockatoo *Cacatua sulphurea.* Some of these birds were offered to us as well. I am sure that many birds are still traded in this manner today.

The status of Eclectus parrots in the wild is for the most part secure. The main threat is the deforestation of habitat, which is still carried out at an alarming rate. All wildlife, not just birds, will decline if they have no place to breed.

6. Biak Island Eclectus, *Eclectus roratus biaki.*

Found on the island of Biak, the Biak Island Eclectus parrot *Eclectus roratus biaki* is smaller than the Red sided *Eclectus roratus polychloros.* Both male and female are brighter in appearance than the red sided: the male is a deep forest green, his beak is a dark rich orange color and has a trace of yellow to the tip of his tail.

The female has a bright red head and breast, the bib is a deep blue with a trace of lavender, her beak is shiny black, and her tail feathers are a darker red than the female *Eclectus roratus polychloros*.

Biak Island is in Cenderawasih (Geelvink) Bay off the northern coast of West Papua, formally West Irian. It is 45 miles (72 km) long and 23 miles (37 km) wide and with a total land area of 948 square miles (2,455 km). Biak town where the main airport is located is the largest town. Garuda (Indonesian) airlines used to have a stopover at Biak on its Los Angeles to Jakarta flight and there were plans to reinstate it. There are many bird watching tours originating from Biak town to Yapen and other islands as well as the mainland.

This sub species would have to be the most adorable member of this fascinating group of birds. When you see a pair of these birds sitting together, they are like jewels glittering in the morning sunshine, their feathers so brilliant they seem to sparkle.

In 1991, a Christian missionary imported a total of fifteen Eclectus parrots into the United States of America, among them were thirteen *Eclectus roratus biaki*. The rest were *Eclectus roratus polychloros;* these birds legally imported into the U.S.A. were then sold, presumably to raise funds for the Christian mission back on Biak.

A few of the pairs of Biak island Eclectus that entered the U.S.A. back in 1991 have at least finished up in the hands of some of the top Eclectus breeders in that country, notably Laurella Desborough, of Florida, and Susie Christian in California. One of the original owners of these pairs Mr. Mike Emani started a studbook for this sub species. But with a limited gene pool and a small number of breeding pairs it will require a concerted effort to produce enough genetically diverse birds to maintain a pure strain of this sub species. All owners and breeders of Biak Island Eclectus should be encouraged to work together in captive breeding and species management programs to insure the long-term survival of this unique sub species.

According to Laurella Desborough, the Biaki Island Eclectus parrot appear to be most closely related to the Red Sided Eclectus *Eclectus roratus polychloros,* rather than the Solomon Island Eclectus *Eclectus roratus solomonensis,* based on the colors of the male and the behavior of both male and female. The ritual behaviors of both sub species are similar, but the basic sub species behaviors of the Biaki Island Eclectus are more like those of the Red Sided Eclectus than the Solomon Island Eclectus.

7. New Guinea Eclectus *Eclectus roratus polychloros.*

The New Guinea Eclectus *Eclectus roratus polychloros* would have to be the most popular Eclectus parrot sub species kept in aviculture today. Also known as the Red Sided Eclectus parrot, this sub species is the most popular because it is the most common, and of all the nine sub species, this New Guinea sub species has the widest range.

Found throughout mainland New Guinea, both on the West Papua and Papua New Guinea sides of the border, this sub species is widely distributed on the Kai Islands in the Arafura Sea, Trobriand Island which lies in the Solomon Sea, and has been introduced to Goram Island and the Palau Islands in the West Pacific Ocean. There are also Eclectus parrots found on the island of Numfor in Cenderawasih (Geelvink) Bay, West Papua. This island was one of the last named islands in this region. In *Birds of New Guinea* by Tom Iredale, 1956, edition, he quotes "Of little importance therefore are the three island races listed, *aruensis* from the Aru Islands, *biaki* from Biak Island, and *maforensis* from Numfor Island." These races all differ only slightly in size, and color variations of the red and blue of the female birds. Also, although not widely known is the existence of a small population (est. 300 birds) of *Eclectus roratus polychloros* on three islands in the Torres Strait. These islands Boigu, Dauan and Saibai are only 4 miles (6.4km) from the Papua New Guinea mainland. These three small islands with a total area of about 100 km² lie in Australian territorial waters and are part of the state of Queensland. *Draffin et al, 1983* states that Eclectus parrots visit these islands on daily foraging trips from breeding and roosting sites on the New Guinea mainland. They have also been seen at hollows in *Pandanus* palms on Saibai Island (*M. Trenerry)* suggesting local breeding.

The male New Guinea Eclectus parrot is a stocky forest green bird of about thirteen to thirteen and a half inches in length, its underwing is bright red and protrudes to the sides of the breast, hence the name "Red Sided." The eye is dark orange/red, the tail feathers are green and black, and with deep blue along the center, the tail is tipped with pale yellow to about 3/8th of an inch.

Female New Guinea Eclectus parrots are also stocky in appearance, they are bright red and have a royal blue breast, and the royal blue extends to the nape of the neck, forming a narrow collar. The back and upper wing coverts are a deep maroon. The under tail coverts are red, and the tail feathers are dark red with a brighter red tip. The eyes are creamy white and also have the blue feathers surrounding the eyes.

The New Guinea Eclectus parrot were possibly the first sub species to come into aviculture, kept widely throughout the world today and is bred in large numbers both in the United Kingdom and in the United States of America. The New Guinea Eclectus parrot is also very popular here in Australia, although like the U.K. and the U.S.A. many birds are crossbred with the Solomon Island Eclectus *Eclectus roratus solomonensis,* and are therefore hard for the inexperienced breeder to identify.

During the 1950s the late Sir Edward Hallstrom, who at that time was the Director of Taronga Park Zoological Gardens in Sydney, Australia, imported many bird species to add to the collection at the Zoo. Quite a few species came from New Guinea and the Solomon Islands, among these shipments were Eclectus parrots. Sir Edward who lived at Northbridge, a Sydney suburb, also had a private Zoo at Mona Vale, a beachside suburb to the north of Sydney where he would go on weekends. As a teenager I used to ride my pushbike from Dee Why, about fourteen miles closer to Sydney than Mona Vale, to work at Sir Edward's private Zoo.

Sir Edward Hallstrom had a beautiful collection of birds housed in some large and ornate aviaries, some even better and bigger than the ones at Taronga Zoo. Sir Edward was in my view more of a collector than an aviculturist and had many pairs of the same species.

While I was working there on one of those weekends, a truck arrived from the city with some shipping crates of birds. I was told to help unload them and release them into empty aviaries that had been prepared for them during the preceding week. One of the other workmen who was the foreman for Sir Edward told me they were birds from New Guinea. There were two crates containing bird of paradise. These were to be acclimatized here before going to Taronga Zoo, where they were to be housed in new aviaries that were being built for them. In the other crates were some other bird species that I did not know and two crates of Eclectus parrots. From the writing on the box I could see that they came from Port Moresby, New Guinea and Honiara, in the Solomon Islands. These birds were all released together into one large flight aviary.

Many of the Eclectus parrots we have today here in Australia, originated from this gene pool of birds imported during the 1950s for Sir Edward Hallstrom and Taronga Zoo, resulting in many crossbred birds. In the late 1950s the importation of birds (except for Zoos) was banned.

The New Guinea Eclectus parrot has been introduced to the Island Republic of Palau in the Western Pacific Ocean, about 340 islands. Palau forms the western end of the Caroline Island chain. Palau's major populated islands are Babelthuap, Koror, Malakal, Arakabesan and Peleliu all of which lie within a single barrier reef covering a 489 square mile area.

Palau Island is very tropical and has an annual rainfall of 150 inches (3800mm) per year; these islands are very fertile, with mangrove swamps around the coast, backed by open forest, coconut and pandanus palms rising to thick rainforest on the hills. The birds of Palau are reported to be in abundance and colourful, with many migratory birds visiting these islands twice a year.

8. Solomon Island Eclectus *Eclectus roratus solomonensis.*

The Solomon Island Eclectus *Eclectus roratus solomonensis* is the most easterly found member of all the Eclectus sub species, found throughout the Islands of Guadalcanal, New Georgia, Malaita, Santa Isabel, San Cristobal and Choiseul. This group of islands lies to the east of Papua New Guinea in the Pacific Ocean. This sub species is also found on Bougainville, New Britain, New Ireland and the Admiralty Islands and throughout the Bismarck Archipelago.

Solomon Island Eclectus parrots are smaller than their New Guinea neighbour *Eclectus roratus polychloros* being about twelve inches (32 cm) in length. The male Solomon Island is a short stocky bird with only a short four-inch tail; this tail is tipped with about 3/8 inch of pale yellow. When the bird sits in its natural position the wing tips almost touch the tip of the tail. The green feathers of the male have a yellow tinge through them. The beak is a paler orange with a yellow tip; the eyes are orange/red similar to those of the New Guinea Eclectus parrot.

The female Solomon Island Eclectus is a deeper red than the *Eclectus roratus polychloros*, has creamy white eyes and a more pronounced blue feathering to the orbital eye ring. The blue to the breast is brighter than the royal blue of *Eclectus roratus polychloros* and its red bib is narrower. There is a distinct separation between the red bib and the bright blue breast.

The export numbers of Solomon Island Eclectus from these islands has not been anywhere near the large numbers exported from Indonesia, i.e. the Grand Eclectus *Eclectus roratus roratus* and the Vosmaeri Eclectus *Eclectus roratus vosmaeri* which were exported in considerable numbers during the 1970s and early 1980s. Solomon Island Eclectus parrots are in reasonable numbers in aviculture in the United States of America, Europe and the United Kingdom. Here in Australia, they are few, and pure birds are very hard to find due to cross breeding with the New Guinea Eclectus parrot *Eclectus roratus polychloros*. There are numbers of this sub species in captivity in South Africa and a small number in New Zealand.

As breeders of Eclectus Parrots we should encourage other breeders to produce pure bred birds and to educate the people who purchase these birds to do the same. Ten years ago Eclectus were sold as just "Eclectus" which covered all the sub species in captivity at that time. It's only in the past few years that breeders started to become aware of specific sub species and started to breed pure birds. I would like to encourage all breeders to breed only pure birds, even for the pet bird market, because in time crossbreeding will come back to haunt us all. It is far better to wait and seek out the preferred mate for the sub species you have than waste time, which could run into years, by placing two birds together that are not of the same sub species.

The status of the Solomon Island Eclectus is common throughout its range and would be regarded as secure. The only threat this sub species would possibly have is the threat of deforestation from multinational logging companies, and the current political situation.

9. The Australian Eclectus *Eclectus roratus macgillivrayi.*

This the largest of the Eclectus parrot sub species and is confined to the north eastern corner of Cape York Peninsula, North Queensland, Australia. The Australian Eclectus parrot is the most southern member of the Eclectus group.

Australian Eclectus *Eclectus roratus macgillivrayi* are much larger than their New Guinea neighbor *Eclectus roratus polychloros*. Mainly due to their longer tail, their overall length is just over 16 inches (42 cm) including a 7inch (18 cm) tail. The broadness of the heads of both the male and female are characteristic of this beautiful sub species. The male Australian Eclectus is a bright forest green with a tinge of yellow through the feathers, its beak is a deep coral orange with a brighter yellow tip. The eyes are dark red /orange; the tail is deep dark green on the outer edge and black on the inner edge with a royal blue strip along both sides of the feather shaft. The tail feathers are tipped with about ½ an inch of pale yellow to the center, changing to a bright yellow at the edges.

The Australian Eclectus female is a strikingly beautiful, somewhat majestic looking bird. If you keep the New Guinea Eclectus *Eclectus roratus polychloros* and you have a nice looking female, just imagine that female about half as big again and you will have a somewhat better idea of the size and beauty of these birds. Overall the female Australian Eclectus is a brighter red than *Eclectus roratus polychloros* with a longer tail. The royal blue breast has a paler sky blue edging. This edging is also present on the shoulder and edge of the wing and is more pronounced than it is on *Eclectus roratus polychloros*. The eyes are dark with an orange ring; the blue feathers to the orbital eye ring are similar to *Eclectus roratus polychloros* but not as pronounced as *Eclectus roratus solomonensis*. The seven inch (18 cm) long tail is deep burgundy red on the outer edge beginning at the shaft decreasing to pale red at the tip. The inner edge starts off as a charcoal gray near the shaft changing to a lighter burgundy red then to pale red at the tip. Some feathers from older females have a tendency to show pink to the center of the tail tip.

The total area that Australian Eclectus parrots are found is about the same size as the island of Sumba, where the Cornelia's Eclectus *Eclectus roratus cornelia* are found. Many people not familiar with Australia still believe that the entire east coast is rainforest and that Eclectus are found as far south as Sydney. I recall reading an article in a European bird magazine stating that Eclectus are found throughout Australia.

The Australian Eclectus parrot *Eclectus roratus macgillivrayi* are only found on the eastern side of Cape York Peninsula bounded by the Rocky River to the south and the Pascoe River to the north. Its range extends west to the Peach River and the area east of the town of Coen known as Blue Mountain. There have been reports of Eclectus parrots being sighted around Lake Barrine on the Atherton Tableland and at Cape Tribulation north of Cairns. Forshaw (1969) edition of *Australian Parrots* reports that Austin (1956) states that in August 1955 a group of five parrots were observed 50 km from Lake Barrine. I agree with Forshaw that these birds were escapees from captivity and were the sub species *Eclectus roratus polychloros* as at that time to my knowledge there were no *Eclectus roratus macgillivrayi* in captivity during that period.

The Australian Eclectus Parrot was not described until 1913, when William McLennan discovered this sub species and the Red-Cheeked Parrot *Geoffroyus geoffroyi* in July of that year. Today their status is very secure, as most of their restricted range is now National Park; they are reasonably common throughout their range.

In captivity their numbers are very low, with only about fifty birds registered with the wildlife authorities throughout Australia. There could be a number of *Eclectus roratus macgillivrayi* held by aviculturists who breed *Eclectus roratus polychloros* and have one or two *Eclectus roratus macgillivrayi* among them, but are unaware of the difference between these two sub species. New Guinea Eclectus *Eclectus roratus polychloros* are classified as exotic birds and do not require a license to keep them, except for one or two States where an exotic license is required.

My thirty-two-year involvement with Australian Eclectus Parrots goes back to 1968 when a party of nine of us left Sydney for Cape York Peninsula to film a documentary on Palm Cockatoos *Probosciger aterrimus macgillivrayi*. It was during the eight weeks we spent filming at Iron Range that I began to watch these bright red and almost iridescent green parrots flying through the rainforest. We would see these birds every day, starting at daylight. Eclectus would give us a wakeup call, squawking in their familiar tones. There was a group of five to eight birds every morning near our camp on the middle crossing of the Claudie River. During the day we were building hides near a Palm Cockatoo's nest and preparing to film them, when a flock of Eclectus Parrots would fly in and land in eucalyptus trees quite near to us. This particular day there were only two of us, the cameraman and myself. I was the bird guide and acting soundman that day. The flock of Eclectus were unaware we were there and some great footage was shot of them. These groups of birds were seven males and three females. The area we were in was open forest but close to the rainforest edge. These parrots were feeding on the seeds and flowering buds of the eucalyptus trees.

The Australian Eclectus was a common sight during the eight weeks we spent filming throughout the Iron Range area. Although the purpose of our trip was to film Palm Cockatoos it was not hard to be distracted by these exceptional birds.

On days that we were not filming, either due to overcast days or just a rest day, my wife and daughter and I would spend the best part of the day walking through the rainforest, sometimes venturing into the open forest. It was on one of these days we decided to explore along one of the many tracks that were made by mining companies during the 1950s (Iron Range gets its name from the iron ore deposits that are found there). This track was known locally as the top Pascoe track, as it led to the mouth of the Pascoe River. We were walking along this track that had not had any vehicle traffic since the last dry season. The wet season is from Dec. to Mar. and the dry season is from about May to Nov. so between the months of December through April entry to Cape York north of the town of Coen is not possible due to flooding and boggy tracks.

It's also worth noting that once we left the City of Cairns we had a distance of 471miles (759 km.) to reach Iron Range, which took us four and a half days, and during these four and a half days we had to cross sixty creeks and five major rivers. Each of these creeks and in particular the rivers were flowing at that time of the year (July) and had to be crossed with care using the winch mounted on the front of two of the Land Rovers.

While we were walking along the Pascoe track each mile or so we would come to a small creek. Most of them were already dry but now and then one would be running. Each of these creeks would have pockets of rainforest along the edges spreading out for a hundred meters or so on either side of the creek. Although it was the month of July and winter here in Australia, this far north they don't have winter and summer they just call it the wet and dry season. The temperature was 32°c (90°f.) and the humidity was 98 percent so it was refreshing to take a break and cool off in the rainforest and have a swim in the crystal clear running water of the creek. I had to be always on my guard as we were in crocodile country and the Pascoe River was notorious for them. There were also wild pigs that were common in the north of Australia. Another we had to be aware of was the Taipan snake, Australia's deadliest reptile. One bite from it and there is no time to go for help—in 45 seconds it's over. We saw many on this trip, but thankfully none on that day.

While we were resting in the creek we heard Eclectus Parrots calling about 100 meters away along this creek. The call we heard was a flute like call. We decided to check it out as it may be nesting. What we found was a female working a hollow in a tall fig tree. The nest site was not that high, only about 10 meters or so. We spent about an hour sitting in the cool of the rainforest watching this female. I was told that they did not nest until October, so she must have been preparing this hollow for the coming breeding season.

Just as we were about to leave to return to the others back at our camp, the female made that fluted call again and we heard another bird calling back to her. A few moments later a magnificent large male appeared and landed on a branch close to the nest hollow. The female came out and flew to the male, he regurgitated some food and fed her.

I decided to let the film producer know of this nest as it would be good to film these birds for the documentary. The next day the whole film crew came and set up to capture what my family and I saw the day before. We set up and waited, and waited, no birds showed up, we gave it about three hours, but not one Eclectus parrot was sighted. In fact we did not even hear any in that area that morning. I believe that at this time of year the Eclectus would have quite a few trees such as this one and she was just getting the feel of it before the breeding season started.

Over the course of the next few weeks we came upon many examples of this. We saw Sulphur-crested Cockatoos *Cacatua galerita* and Palm Cockatoos *Prosciger aterrimus macgillivrayi* doing the same thing, excavating nest sites for the coming breeding season.

The sighting of that beautiful pair of Australian Eclectus that day is a sight I will never forget, the stunning red female and the very large fully matured male alighting on that branch and feeding the female, my family and I sitting, trying not to move or make a sound that would frighten them off. The sight of this pair of birds in the shade of the rainforest their colours so brilliant and their feathers hair like was indeed a sight to behold.

Chapter 2
The 1968 Expedition to Cape York

The purpose of this chapter, the 1968 Expedition to Cape York, is to help those keepers and breeders of Eclectus parrots, for whatever reason, may not or will not ever get the chance to see first hand these magnificent parrots in their wild state.

These notes I share with you come from my Cape York Diaries, a collection of journals I kept from bird watching and collecting expeditions to the rainforest of Cape York Peninsula, far northern Queensland, Australia. These expeditions were during the years starting in 1968 and concluding in 1985, a period of eighteen years.

The year was 1967, I was twenty seven years of age, my wife Marcia and I had been married just four years and we had a daughter Lisa who had just had her second birthday. Here was I dreaming of going to Cape York! To search for Palm Cockatoos. Why Palm Cockatoos? I had been breeding birds since I was fifteen years old; I was always a parrot and cockatoo man. My main interest at the time was black cockatoos. We were living on a small two and a quarter acre property at Terrey Hills in one of Sydney's northern suburbs, where we built a small home and about thirty parrot and cockatoo aviaries. The species of black cockatoos I had were Red Tail Black Cockatoo *Calyptorhynchus magnificus samueli*, Yellow Tail Black Cockatoo *Calyptorhynchus funereus funereus,* the White Tailed Black Cockatoo *Calyptorhynchus baudinii latirostris.* I also had pairs of Gang Gang Cockatoos *Callocephalon fimbriatum* and pairs of Major Mitchell

Cockatoos *Cacatua leadbeateri* and Long Billed Corellas *Cacatua tenuirostris.*

The only species of black cockatoos that I did not have set up for breeding were the Glossy Black Cockatoo *Calyptorhynchus lathami* and the Great Palm Cockatoo *Probosciger aterrimus macgillivrayi.* About six months earlier I was offered a pair of Palm Cockatoos from a good friend of mine, Ray Ackroyd. Ray was Sydney's best bird dealer at the time. He also was a professional bird trapper and had licenses to trap the non protected species of parrots and cockatoos throughout the states of N.S.W., Victoria and South Australia.

Ray Ackroyd would probably be the best bird man I have ever met. I purchased my very first parrots from him when I was about fifteen. They were a pair of Superb Parrots *Polytelis swainsonii.* Ray and I are still mates to this day.

When I received a phone call from him offering me the pair of Palm Cockatoos he also offered me a pair of Blue and Gold Macaws *Ara ararauna.* Ray, who I would visit at least every second weekend, knew I was interested in developing a bird park someday and these were the species of birds I was after. At that time I could not afford both pairs, Ray expected me to take the Palms, but I decided to take the pair of Blue and Golds. My reasoning for this was I wanted to collect my own Palm Cockatoos from the wild as I would have a much better understanding of how to care for them if I studied them in their natural habitat. Little did I know then that in a few years I would get that chance?

The following weekend Ray arrived with the pair of Macaws. We released them into their new aviary, which was thirty feet long by eight feet high and six feet wide; they seemed to settle in well. Marcia prepared morning tea for us, and we sat and watched the Macaws. During our conversation Ray mentioned that an American by the name of Robert Nelson had called into his bird shop and had a problem with his pet white cockatoo, and would he mind if he came out and saw me as I might be able to help him, I said that would be okay.

Late on the Sunday afternoon a car drove into our driveway. A couple got out and introduced themselves as Robert and Mary Nelson. We talked and I asked them if they would like to see my birds, they said they would love to.

As we walked around the birds they were amazed at what species I had, especially the cockatoos. They were taken by the condition of my birds and asked what I fed them, I said I'm a great believer in feeding as much natural food as I could and as we lived next to a large national park it was not hard to collect Casuarina Nuts *Casurina stricta* and this we would do about twice a week. These were fed to all the cockatoos.

Mr. Nelson then brought up the subject of his cockatoos, and asked me if I could take a look at them. I said I was told you only have the one bird. No I have four, he said. I asked what was the problem with them and when did he want to bring them out so I could take a look at them. He said I have them in the car and we walked over to where they were parked. I did not remember seeing any birds when they drove up. He opened the door and here was this metal box about four feet long and sixteen inches wide on the back seat, we pulled this carrying box out which was divided into five compartments. There was one cockatoo to each compartment, and one that was empty. All the birds were in various stages of feather plucking, one was almost completely naked.

After looking at each of his birds, I said I'm afraid I have only bad news. These birds have what I am sure was beak and feather disease and I cannot let you bring them any closer to my birds. He went silent for a few minutes and asked if I was sure. I said I would give him the name of my vet who was an experienced avian veterinarian, take the birds to him and he will advise you of what you should do. What do you think he will do, he asked me. I said sorry but if the birds have beak and feather they will have to be put down, this disease is highly contagious and should be dealt with now.

I gave him the phone number of my vet. And they left. It was not the best way to meet new friends but I had very little choice. About three weeks later the Nelsons called in to see us; he thanked me for my help and for the name of my vet. He said the birds did have beak and feather and were put down. I said that I was sorry but there was no other way.

He asked if they could have another look at my birds as they had not seen black cockatoos before and wanted to have another look. As we walked around the aviaries we were talking about black cockatoos and I said that next year (1968) we were going to do an expedition to Cape York searching for the Great Palm Cockatoo. Robert Nelson then asked what do they look like, I went inside and got my copy of *What Bird is That* by Neville Cayley, the 1959 edition which had colour plates of all Australian birds. I showed him the plate of the palm cockatoo and the other birds found in Cape York. I said that to my knowledge palm cockatoos in Australia had not been photographed before. He asked me if they had been filmed. I said not that I'm aware of. He then said your trip would make a good documentary film and asked would we be interested in having a film crew tag along. I said it was really just a private bird watching trip as the secret to good bird keeping was understanding what their requirements were in the wild and translate that to their life in captivity.

This was the practice of mine with the black cockatoos. Each time I planned a new sub species for my breeding collection I would spend as much time as I could in their natural environment, watching what they ate, where they nested, how long the chick stayed in the nest, the depth of the nest log even down to the type of tree they nested in. All these facts are so important to good bird keeping. I am sure using this method is one of the main reasons I was credited with the first breeding in captivity of the White-tailed Black Cockatoo *Calyptorhynchus funereus latirostris* in 1971.

I said that we would think about it and let him know, and he left. My wife and I talked about it for a while then forgot all about it. About six weeks later the phone rang and Mr. Nelson wanted to come out on the weekend and bring someone out with him. I said that would be fine, see you next Sunday. They came out and he introduced his friend to us, his name was Bill Eve, and he was going to be the director/soundman on the trip, if we decided that we would like to have a film crew along. I said we had thought about it and as we did not have much of the detail we were willing to talk about it. Over the course of the next few weeks there were many meetings and discussions about our planned trip. Before we knew it the size of party grew from just my wife, daughter and myself to a party of nine: two Americans, one German and six Australians.

The deciding factor for my wife and I to agree to this trip was it was well sponsored by some of the leading companies in this country, namely Rover Australia who provided the five four wheel drive Land Rovers, plus service and spare parts, Masterfoods Pty.Ltd who supplied all the one and a half tons of tin food, and the Shell Petroleum Co. who supplied all the fuel and oil for this expedition, plus the many other smaller companies that provided us with three flat bottom aluminium boats, outboard motors and two trail motorbikes, camping gear etc. etc. When all this equipment was displayed on the front lawn of our property for the media press release two weeks before we left for North Queensland, I wasn't sure it would all fit in the five vehicles provided.

On the 16th of July 1968 we departed Sydney in the convoy of five vehicles for Iron Range Cape York Peninsula. The route out of Sydney took us due West over the Blue Mountains into the western plains of outback New South Wales. We should have been heading due North but we wanted to shoot some scenes of the Australian outback on our way to Queensland.

We reached the town of Bourke on the Darling River in Far Western N.S.W.

And turned north for Queensland.

The distance from Sydney to Iron Range if we took the most direct route up the Pacific Highway (National Route One) was a total for the round trip of 3906 miles (6290 km). The route we decided to take through the western plains of outback N.S.W. and Queensland would add another 1000 miles or so to the trip.

We traveled through the country towns of Cunnamulla, Charleville, Augathella, Blackall, Barcaldine, Muttaburra, Torrens Creek then headed due East for the coast through the town of Charters Towers then onto the Coastal City of Townsville. Each night we would camp out near a creek or dam so we had water for a swim or a good wash. From the time we left the town of Bourke we were traveling on dusty dirt roads and in some cases tracks covered in bull dust. This is fine gray dust that looks and feels like talcum powder and gets in everything.

Bob Nelson led our party for the first two days after leaving Sydney, but would not stop early enough in the afternoon daylight to set up a proper camp. After the second night when he stopped at 11pm in pouring rain we demoted him as leader and I took over. From then on we would start looking for a campsite at 5pm and have enough time to set up tents and cook a hot meal; from then on we had a happy crew.

From Townsville it was only a half day's drive up the Bruce Highway to the Far North Queensland City of Cairns, gateway to the Great Barrier Reef. We were all excited about having a swim at Ellis Beach, where we would camp for a few days to take stock, have the vehicles serviced and any repairs needed, replenish our supplies and generally have a rest. Bob wanted to send the footage back to Sydney to be processed so he could have a look at the film we had shot on our way here.

Everyone enjoyed the stay at Ellis Beach, which is fourteen miles north of Cairns along the Captain Cook Highway, its tropical beaches lined with palm trees and the pure white sand. It was hard to load up the vehicles again and leave. The night before we left Cairns Bob called us all together to view the footage we had shot earlier, which arrived back from Sydney that afternoon. We all agreed it looked great. Some of the scenes of the vehicles bogged in the muddy black soil country of western Queensland and driving through lots of bull dust were to me exciting stuff.

But the real excitement lay ahead of us. The next morning we packed up early and were on the road north again by eight am. Our convoy was now six Land Rovers, as the large studio van, which carried most of the heavy film equipment, was too heavy and too high to make it through to Iron Range. So on the advice of the local office of the department of main roads, Bob decided to put the van on the ship that delivered the monthly supplies to the Aboriginal mission at Lockhart River near where we hoped to be camped. All the film equipment we needed for the 471 mile (759 km) trip further north was loaded on the new vehicle.

The convoy headed north along the Captain Cook Highway. We had a nice view of the ocean all the way to Port Douglas and the sugar milling town of Mossman. A short distance south of Mossman we turned west up and over the Great Dividing Range to the small mining town of Mount Molloy, then it was north again along the road towards Cooktown. The road was still bitumen but the further north we went the narrower it became. It was just one lane now and when large transport trucks were coming towards you there was only one thing to do and that was to get off the bitumen otherwise you couldn't see for the dust and if you weren't careful either hit the transport truck or run off the road.

A few miles further the bitumen finished. From here on it would be a dusty road until we returned back the way we came in two months time. We stopped at the Butchers Hill turnoff, which is now known as Lakeland Downs cattle station. There was a roadhouse there and we all enjoyed a nice cup of tea and a short break. We refueled all the vehicles, I called all the crew together and told them that we would turn off the Cooktown road and would now be heading up the center of

Cape York Peninsula and there were only two small towns that we could get anything we may have forgotten to get in Cairns. I also said we would be traveling in crocodile and venomous snake country and not to take any risks as the nearest hospital or medical help was at the town of Coen, which would be the last town we would see for the next two months or so.

On the maps that I was using these roads were called developmental roads. It was one of the roughest roads I had ever traveled, and the dustiest. When we were a few miles south of the town of Laura we started to notice a formation of rocky hills with large sandstone cliffs. These sandstone cliffs, as we found out later, contained many Aboriginal cave paintings. As our convoy arrived at the town of Laura we were surrounded by a group of Aboriginal children who seemed very interested in our arrival. Laura is a very small town. It consisted of a pub, a store and maybe six or seven houses, and the store also sold fuel. Outside the pub were large mango trees where we sat to wait our turn at the fuel pump, the refueling of the six vehicles took over an hour because the fuel pump was a hand pump as there was no electricity. We had now really reached the outback of Australia.

Bob Nelson decided to film the town and the refueling of the vehicles. We also shot scenes of us buying supplies from the store. This store was rather unique as it was the first store I had been in that had an earth floor. The local people were so friendly and were keen to get on camera. We were all invited into the pub for a drink, the publican was Percy Trezise who discovered the cave paintings south of town. He asked if we would like to film them. Bob said we would like to very much. During the discussions about these cave paintings Percy told us he had discovered them while flying over them. Percy was a pilot for Ansett Airlines that had the twice weekly flight from Cairns to Coen and then on to Weipa, the bauxite mining town on the coast of the Gulf of Carpentaria.

It was on these flights that over the years he would sit in the cockpit with an aerial survey map on his lap and mark the position of likely areas that could reveal more rock paintings. Then when he had a few days off he would drive up from Cairns to Laura, pick up his good mate Dick Roughsey, a local Aboriginal tracker, and then head off to look for these rocky outcrops he had seen from the air.

In the eighteen years that I have been coming back to Cape York, each trip I would call into Laura, catch up with Percy and Dick and get the latest update on the cave paintings. At last count they had discovered over 300 separate areas containing rock or cave paintings. The last time I saw Percy he had retired from flying and was living at Laura and conducted tours to his beloved paintings.

After spending the next day filming the cave paintings at a place called Split Rock with Percy we returned to our camp at the Laura River just south of the town.

Early the next morning we were on the road again. Next stop was the town of Coen, which would be our last town for some two months. The track was only a single vehicle width and in places soft sand. Most people even here in Australia think that the whole of Cape York is jungle and rainforest and do not expect it to be dry and dusty. In fact there is very little rainforest and it's all on the East Coast side of the cape. There were fragments of rainforest on each side of some of the rivers and the larger creeks that we crossed and at this time of the year which was just the start of the dry season most of these creeks and rivers were running. In fact from the turn off at Lakeland Downs to Iron Range we crossed sixty creeks and five major rivers in a distance of 471 miles (759 km). This distance also took us five days to cover.

Our next camp was on the Hann River. Percy had told us of a good camp site that only the locals knew. We would have to turn off to the right after we crossed the river and head along the river for two miles where we would come to a clearing. We drove to this clearing and here was this great camping site where there were small waterfalls and crystal clear pools bounding with wildlife. A large flock of Red-tailed Black Cockatoos *Calyptorhynchus magnificus magnificus* flew from where they were feeding on the ground near the edge of the river. They stayed in the area until just before dark, when they all took off as one. It was quite a sight; their bright red tails a deep red orange in the late afternoon sunlight. I could not help myself when I looked at the two Americans and Hans the German guy: all three of them were standing there with their mouths open, as if to say why we didn't get that on film. I said don't worry we will get them in the morning, which we did.

We set up camp and we stayed there for two days. We filmed a lot of scenes in on and around the river. Bob also took some good shots of some of the wildlife we found in the area. Some of the species we saw were Blue-cheeked Rosella, *Platycercus adscitus adscitus*, and Red-winged Parrot *Aprosmictus erthropterus coccineopterus*; there were plenty of Galahs *Eolophus roseicapillus* and Little Corellas *Cacatua pastinator normantoni* sighted along the road after leaving the town of Laura.

I spent hours scouting for the film crew. Late on the second afternoon after we had finished filming a large Monitor Lizard and we were walking along a dry creek bed back towards our camp, I caught a movement out of the corner of my eye. I said stop to Bob and Richard the cameraman who were just ahead of me. They stopped and I pointed to the small clump of bush about three feet in front of them. There under the bush was a Taipan, Australia's most dangerous snake. It was at least seven-feet in length. Bob tried to insist that I shoot it, but I said no, if we leave it alone it will leave us alone. Anyway I said Taipans are very shy and the only time they will bite you is when you try and interfere with them. They will usually hear you coming and move out of sight. The snake moved on and so did we, although Bob and Richard did not sleep out on the ground with the rest of us that night.

We would see many more reptiles before this trip was over. Early the next morning we loaded the vehicles and headed north again following the telegraph line, which was the communication phone line between

Cairns and Thursday Island in the Torres Strait. Along this track there were many termite mounds. Some of them were only three feet or so high and a sandy color. Others were over ten feet high and a rich red earth color; there was also the wide narrow type that they called the magnetic termite mound. This was because they always faced north and south. We crossed the Morehead River, which was about 300 yards wide, and running about two feet at the first crossing then there was a sand bar in the middle of the river before crossing a second time; the second crossing was not as deep.

Each time we came to a major river such as the Morehead, one of us would walk across first. This way we had a much better idea of where the deep water was. All the vehicles crossed without any problems. The weather was hot and not a cloud in the sky. It did not take long to get all sweaty and each time we came to one of these rivers or creeks we would all rush in for a quick dip, fully clothed in most cases, because you would be dry within half an hour.

We arrived at Musgrave Station (in Australia, a cattle ranch is called a station) which was one of the largest cattle stations in the Cape. As the convoy drove up towards the homestead we noticed a group of horses close to the wire fence. One of the foals had its leg tangled in the wire fence and was lying on the ground. Peter Schreck, who was roustabout for our crew, knew about horses and was quickly out of his vehicle and covered the foal's head with his shirt, while I retrieved a pair of wire cutters from our tool box and cut the wire from the leg. Bob and Richard alerted the station owner who was having his afternoon nap on the veranda. He came down and thanked us for cutting the foal loose. He returned to the homestead to get something to put on the wound, and soon the foal was up and running with its mother again.

The station owner invited us all in for a cup of tea, and we stayed for an hour or so. Many of the homesteads are built off the ground, sitting on wooden posts. This is for two reasons: the first in case of flooding, and the second for coolness, also the ground floor area doubles as a shaded work area. As the station owner showed us around we told him the reason for our trip. He then said he wanted to show us something under the homestead. We followed him downstairs past all the saddles, bridles and riding gear to the back corner of the building where he had a small aviary. In this aviary among dozen or so budgies were five small parrots. I recognized them right away, they were Golden-shouldered Parrots *Psephotus chysopterygius,* one of Australia's rarest parrots.

In captivity the Golden-shouldered Parrot was in limited numbers in the southern states of Victoria and New South Wales, but was fully protected in its home range state of Queensland. So I was not expecting to see any in captivity on this trip. The station owner told us that these birds were rescued during the cattle muster at the end of the wet season last year. These parrots nest in the termite mounds we saw on our way in that day and when the cattle are mustered these termite mounds are often knocked over by the cattle. These birds were rescued by one of the stationhands. He said they would be released when old enough to fend for themselves.

We thanked him for having us all for afternoon tea and the information he gave us about the state of the road north to Coen, and for letting us see the rare parrots.

The convoy drove off across the airfield to the crossroads and turned north. The area around Musgrave Station is what we call black soil country here in Australia. It's very dusty in the dry season but can be impassable in the wet as it just turns to bog. I was on the lookout now for Golden-shouldered Parrots as this time of year was their breeding season. There were thousands of termite mounds but I saw no Golden-shouldered Parrots.

The town of Coen is somewhat larger than Laura. We arrived there late in the afternoon, drove up along the 100-meter strip of bitumen, where well presented houses were on either side of the road. Again our convoy attracted all the locals outside to see what the fuss was all about. We lined up at the fuel pump, and then we all went into the store. One thing you quickly realize when traveling in the outback of this country is that everything is so laid back, nothing is or becomes a problem and everyone expects you to take the time to have a chat with them. Before long we were all sitting at the table under the shop veranda having a cup of tea with Mrs. Taylor (no relation) who owned the only store and guesthouse in the town. We had fresh baked scones and Anzac biscuits which to all of us was indeed a treat.

There was quite a group of people sitting with us, half the town it looked like to us. Mrs.Taylor's son asked Bob what we were going to Iron Range for. Bob told him that we wanted to film the Palm Cockatoos and other native parrots that we hoped to find there. He said that there were Palm Cockatoos at the Archer River which was about 40 miles (62 km) north of the town. He said he had often seen them while mustering cattle near Blue Mountain, which he then stood up and pointed to. In the distance I could see a row of hills covered in rainforest. I said do you mean those hills there, and he said yes. I quickly got out my Army survey map and asked him to point it out again on my map which he did. I also made notes in my diary. We stayed there a couple of hours, but the sun was starting to set and we wanted to make it to the Archer River before dark.

We promised them we would call in on the way back and spend a few days filming the town and the locals. Mrs.Taylor said that the Coen races were on in a few weeks and hundreds of people from all over the Cape would be there. These races are only held once a year and it's a great place to meet people that live on some of the remotest cattle stations in CapeYork.

As we drove the short distance to the Archer River along what you could best call a sandy track, I could not help thinking about seeing a Palm Cockatoo in the wild for the first time. The wildlife I had noticed was becoming a common sight, large Kangaroos were trying to commit suicide by running across the road right in front of us— we had to slow down or hit them. They can do a lot of damage to a vehicle and themselves. Groups of Emus would race alongside of us. Bob and

Richard got some wonderful footage of this by sitting on the front of the Land Rover. Small flocks of Red-tailed Black Cockatoos *Calyptorhynchus magnificus macrorhynchus* and Blue-cheeked Rosella *Platycercus adscitus adscitus* were often seen, plus many species of birds of prey.

We stopped on the southern bank of a wide clear running river. It was just on dusk, and we had to find a good campsite before dark so we split up into pairs and looked for a suitable spot for the night. A nice camping site was found in the middle of the river. This river was the widest we had came across so far. It was about 800 meters wide running in three separate channels with large very smooth granite boulders everywhere. There were two large sand bars and trees in the middle of this crossing where someone had camped the night before. We decided that we could fit all the vehicles in off the track.

This camp at the Archer River was one of the best we have had so far on this trip, with its white sandy bottom and clear water which most of us stayed in until late that night. The water was cool at first but after a while was very refreshing; everybody slept well that night.

Next morning I was up at first light and went for a walk down river. I saw my first crocodile, it was a small fresh water type called the Johnston's River Crocodile *Crocodylus johnstoni*. These were harmless and mainly fed on fish. The saltwater crocodile *Crocodylus porosus* or "Saltie" as the locals called them were in this river as well so we had to be careful. Swimming in the shallow holes near our camp was safe as long as we were alert. I was told by one of the locals back in Coen that professional croc shooters took over 700 skins from this river two years ago, but much closer to the river's mouth which was in the Gulf.

On a sand bar in the middle of the river I saw three Dingo's feeding on a carcass of a kangaroo. They were beautiful looking dogs. They were unaware of me watching them, so I decided to return to our camp and let Bob know about them.

While I was walking back I heard my first Palm Cockatoo call. I was a little unsure but it sure sounded like their call, a squawk followed by a long whistle. The section of the river where I was was covered with large paperbark trees. I could not see above the tree tops, so I ran up the bank of the river to see if I could get a better look. The cockatoo had landed in a tree quite a distance ahead of me and was calling. As I got closer I caught my first glimpse of these magnificent cockatoos. It was sitting high in a dead tree in the morning sunlight. If only I had had a cameraman or a camera to capture the sight of this bird. I watched for a while then suddenly it was gone. That first sighting really made my day.

On my return to camp I told Bob and the rest of the crew about the Dingos and my first sighting of the Palm Cockatoo. They said they never heard or saw anything. Bob decided we should go and set up and try and get some footage of the Dingos, I said it would be better if we left it an hour or so to make sure they are back as they may have heard me leave.

We did some other shots along the river well away from where the Dingos were. After lunch we went and set up a hide close to where the kangaroo carcass on the sand bar was. We waited and about 20 minutes later I heard a flapping sound, I touched Bob on the shoulder and indicated to Richard to get ready to shoot. A huge Wedge-tailed Eagle *Aquila audax* landed about two meters from the carcass; these birds of prey are Australian's largest, with a wing span of two to three meters. Another landed and they started feeding. A few moments later from the other side of the river came the pack of Dingos. They must have been watching and waiting like us but once they saw the Eagles eating their kill they decided to protect it. We shot some great footage that day.

We stayed two more days at the Archer River and in that time not one vehicle went past our camp. The track passed right through our camp site and it was the only road north to the tip of Cape York and south back to Coen. I know a few in the crew were starting to wonder what they had gotten themselves into, but for me the more isolated we became the better I liked it.

It would be another ten days before we would see another vehicle on this track.

Our convoy departed the Archer River early the next morning without hearing or seeing any more Palm Cockatoos. We had forty-two miles (67 km) before we had to turn right off the main track onto another track that should take us east towards the coast. When we reached this turnoff there was no sign post and the track looked like it had not been used for quite some time. I checked my map and the trip meter in my vehicle. This had to be it, so off we headed along this track. According to my map we would come to a large river, and if we did, this would be the right track to Iron Range and the coast.

An hour later we were all relieved when we reached the western bank of the Wenlock River. This river was the first one that we encountered that had very steep sandy banks on both sides, it was also running quite deep and care had to be taken to cross it without flooding the vehicles and our gear.

Bob and Richard decided to film our attempts at crossing this river, Hans and I walked across to check the depth and the state of the river bottom, the deepest part was up to our waist and the current was moving quite fast but not strong enough to trouble the Land Rovers. The bottom of the river was sand but not to soft. We returned to the rest of the crew and I told them how we were going to cross. I decided to drive one of the Land Rovers across first that had a winch attached, this way the ones who had not made a crossing like this before could watch where I drove and at what speed. And when I got across if any of the following vehicles got stuck I could winch them out. I told them all that they should be in low range and drive slowly, but do not stop, just drive at a steady pace.

The vehicle that I drove across was very heavy as it carried most of our fuel supply. I put it into low range and started down the steep sandy bank. Bob and Richard were set up with two cameras, one at water level and the other on top of one of the Land Rovers. Getting down the bank was okay and the first part of the river was not too deep. I was about halfway across when the front wheel dipped into a hole and I stopped, but thankfully the motor was still running, I had to back up a bit and then drive around the hole. I made the other side, but had trouble getting enough speed to make it up the steep bank. After about three goes I was up the other side.

I walked back across the river, stuck a branch to mark the spot where the hole was and told the others to cross one at a time. They crossed without any problems except the last one tried to drive too fast and stalled their vehicle in the deepest part of the river. We winched it out, and all vehicles were safely across. Bob was very happy with what he and Richard had got on film and said it's time for lunch. We drove a short distance to the old Wenlock mining camp that was marked on my map; it was deserted now but was a thriving gold mine thirty years ago.

There were a couple of rusty tin sheds, and an old steam driven crusher plant and plenty of odds and ends lying about. There was still gold to be found but not in the quantity that could support a small mining town. We had lunch and spent an hour or so fossicking around the old sheds and the rubbish heaps where there were some interesting old bottles to be found.

The track that would take us to the coast started to become a lot rougher as we began to climb over the Sir William Thompson Range; this range was part of the Great Dividing Range, which runs along the entire east coast of Australia. We were constantly changing from four-wheel drive to low range to make it across some of the gullies and washouts. At one stage we were stopped by a deep washout at the bottom of a steep winding bend in a dry creek. There was no way across or around this obstacle in front of us. All the vehicles stopped and we surveyed the problem that confronted us. The only thing we could do was to cut some trees down, cut them into logs and place them across the washout and hope it would support the weight of the vehicles.

Bob went and got the chainsaw and the rest of us got shovels and bow saws, we proceeded to cut some small trees, trim off the branches and carried them to the gully, after an hour or so we thought it was safe enough to support the Land Rovers. Each one in turn crossed and we were again on our way.

Once we had crossed the range and descended into open forest country again we started to cross many creeks, and according to my map we would soon come to the Pascoe River. The Pascoe River was special to me as an aviculturist; it's all I have read about in the bird books and the research material that I studied before making this trip. Many of the early sightings of the species we wanted to film were made along or near the Pascoe River, and I for one could not wait until we sighted this river.

It was late afternoon when we arrived at the Pascoe, I told Bob and the rest of the crew that we would camp here tonight. Bob and a couple of the others wanted to press on. Just then three Palm Cockatoos flew over our heads which soon changed their minds. We drove the vehicles just off the track in case someone wanted to get past, my wife Marcia and our daughter Lisa and I were off after the cockatoos.

This section of the Pascoe River was about a third of the way from its source at the foot of Mount Tozer, which was the gateway to Iron Range; it was a clear running river with white coarse sand and smooth granite boulders. There were many flowering bottlebrush trees *Grevillea* spp. In and along the river, there were many species of honeyeaters along with Rainbow Lorikeets *Trichoglossus haematodus moluccanus* feeding on these blossoms; it was a great place to camp for the night.

We did not find the three Palm Cockatoos that flew overhead, but we made our first sighting of the rare Red-cheeked Parrot *Geoffroyus geoffroyi aruensis*. It was sitting calling in a dead tree high above the canopy of the forest. It was a male, distinguished by its peach coloured head and was clearly visible in the sunlight. We were to see many more Red-Cheeks on this trip.

The entire crew spent a lazy hour just before sunset lying in the shallows of the Pascoe, enjoying a quiet beer that we had placed in the river to cool. After a nice meal we all sat around the campfire and reflected on our trip thus far.

I was up at daylight, as I wanted to spend as much time along the river as I could, before we moved on, I knew Bob and the film crew wanted to get to our destination and start filming, also the boat from Cairns with the studio truck onboard would be due in a few days. As I was walking upstream in the early mist that was rising off the river; I could hear cockatoos calling again. But these did not sound like Palm Cockatoos. I traveled about another kilometer, then heard them again, they sounded like Sulphur-crested Cockatoos *Cacatua galerita galerita,* but their call was different. As I came to a pocket of open forest I could see these white cockatoos, I focused my binoculars on them, they were smaller than *Cacatua galerita,* and could they be *Cacatua galerita fitzroyi*? I noted this in my diary and their location on my map.

On my return to camp all the others were just finishing breakfast and were starting to pack up. An hour later we were heading east again.

We seemed to be traveling on top of the ranges, we could see mountain peaks on both sides of us, also the forest was more open and there was no rainforest except on these mountain peaks. About an hour passed and we started to descend down this slippery clay or loam based track that had many gutters created by the wet season running along the middle of this track. It was becoming obvious to us that we must be the first vehicles to travel this track since the end of the wet season three months ago.

The Land Rover carrying our fuel slipped into one of these gutters and it took us half an hour to winch it out; we must be fairly close to the coast because it was now a lot more humid than it was earlier. We stopped at Brown's Creek, which was the last crossing before we passed through Tozers Gap. Brown's Creek was more like a river than a creek; it was very rocky and fast flowing and for this time of year quite deep. We stopped and had morning tea, checked the vehicles. I had a chance to check the area for birdlife.

The forest around this creek was semi rainforest with thick open forest on both sides. I heard Red-cheeked Parrots again and also Palm Cockatoos calling some distance away.

The convoy set off again; soon we would pass through Tozers Gap and descend down the range to the Claudie River. Once past Tozers Gap there is a change in the climate. We are now entering thick rainforest, the temperature is cooler but a lot more humid than it was an hour or so earlier.

Passing through this green jungle are many running creeks and rivers. There is a major difference, which is not apparent at first, but once you have gathered your thoughts you realize that all the bird calls are different. You are now hearing the birds of the rainforest.

According to some of Australia's earlier bird books there are some twenty-eight species of birds that are only found in this area bounded by the Rocky River to the south and the Pascoe River to the north and west to Mount Tozer. Among these are the Eclectus Parrot *Eclectus roratus macgillavrayi,* Marshall's Fig Parrot *Cyclopsitta diophthalma marshalli.* The most common birdcall heard during our stay in the rainforest was a long drawn out whistle. It took me a few days to locate who was making it, and it sounded like it was coming from a flute, a long call with a high pitched trill at the end. It turned out to be the Magnificent Riflebird *Ptiloris magnificus.*

Riflebirds are members of the Bird of Paradise family. The Magnificent Riflebird, which is also found in New Guinea, is the largest of the three species found in Australia. The other two sub species are the Paradise Riflebird *Ptiloris paradiseus* and the

Victoria's Riflebird *Ptiloris victoriae*. These are endemic to Australia, and are found further south.

The male Magnificent Riflebird is velvet black with an iridescent crown, and has a broad blue-green breastplate. To watch these birds display is a sight to behold. The male will select a single branch, usually an upright dead tree that has been broken off during the last cyclone, where he will sit calling for the female, sometimes for long periods. When a female arrives he holds both his wings up above his head and starts to dance; raising each wing in turn getting faster and faster until the female is attracted for a closer look. Sometimes the female will just look and leave and sometimes he is lucky and she stays and mating takes place. The sight of these Magnificent Riflebirds displaying in the understory of the rainforest in Cape York will remain with me forever.

We arrived at the first crossing of the Claudie River. The track was very slippery and crossing was difficult. Each vehicle had to drive very slowly otherwise the vehicles would slip and slide off the track. On both sides and down the center of this track grew long green guinea grass which hid anything that was to run out in front of you. This grass was as high as the windscreen and every now and then something would race out in front of you, mostly wild pigs, and once three young Cassowaries *Casuarius casuarius* ran along in front of us for some distance before they disappeared into the jungle.

After crossing the middle crossing of the Claudie River we decided to stop for lunch. The rainforest at this point was the thickest, in most cases the only place you could see the sky was by standing in the middle of the track. This particular spot that we decided to stop at would turn out to be one of the most significant places for me, and would keep me returning to this very spot for the next eighteen years.

While the others were finishing lunch I decided to go walkabout and check the rainforest back across the other side of the river. The bird calls were amazing, Magnificent Riflebirds calling everywhere. I came to a huge ficus tree *Ficus albipilla* that was at least 36 meters (120 feet) tall. Shining Starlings *Aplonis metallica* were just starting to build their nest in the canopy of this tree. Migrating from New Guinea these birds nest in colonies in the top of these trees and build dome shaped nest with an entrance at the side. Little did I know then that these birds would be so important to me over the following years?

Also nesting in this tree was a White Goshawk *Accipiter novaehollandiae* that seemed strange to me at the time, as usually other birds would stay away from birds of prey. While I was gazing at these birds I noticed metal spikes sticking out of this tree. They did not start from the base of the tree but about ten meters from the ground. "Someone has climbed this tree before," and if they only used these metal spikes they did it the hard way, what were they after, I thought to myself. I went back to the others and said they should come and have a look at what I found. We all stood in the center of the track and I pointed to the metal spikes. This time I brought my binoculars with me and I inspected the tree. I could see from where we were standing at least two nesting hollows that would be suitable for cockatoos or parrots. I decided to walk in to the base of the tree and give it a tap with a dead branch, after two hefty wacks out flew a female Eclectus parrot.

This was my first sighting of the Eclectus parrot *Eclectus roratus macgillivrayi* and as it was only early August I was not expecting to see them nesting this early.

This female flew around and circled the tree screeching. Her loud cries sent all the Shining Starlings flying and even the White Goshawk took off to see what the fuss was all about. Soon this female Eclectus attracted other Eclectus from all parts of the forest and before we knew it we had at least a dozen of these bright red and beautiful green parrots flying around. It was quite a sight.

Bob and Richard quickly ran back to our camp and got the camera gear. They set up and managed to get some great shots of these birds.

After about half an hour they all settled down and the female Eclectus returned to the nest accompanied by three males. I watched these birds with great interest. They appeared a lot larger than the ones I'd seen in Sydney and they certainly got my attention.

We still had a way to go before we reached our destination at Portland Roads on the coast. Here we could check when the boat from Cairns would dock and the unloading of our equipment would take place. We were all very keen by this time to see the ocean again. The convoy headed out through the rainforest and across the last crossing of the Claudie River. We now were starting to come out into open forest country again and we could smell the salt air from the sea, and to our complete surprise, suddenly we were driving on bitumen, albeit a bit rough and very narrow.

Palm Cockatoos flew past us as we headed for the coast. We came to our first sign post since we left Coen, a road went to our right and the sign said airport and mission and pointed right, the other sign pointed to the coast and said P/Roads. We headed for Portland Roads.

Portland Roads was a small village of four or five houses, mostly retired people from Cairns who were fed up with the city rat race. These people decided to live here where the fishing was good and where there was plenty of peace and quiet.

We parked the vehicles at the end of the jetty and went for a walk while we waited for someone to show themselves, an hour later we decided to go to one of these houses to see if they knew when the boat would dock. We were met by Ross Pope, who was in charge of the jetty. He invited us in for a cup of tea. He then told us the boat was delayed due to the tide and would now be docking in two days time.

Bob decided to set up camp back a few kilometers in the open forest and wait for the boat to arrive. We would do some filming of the port and some of the local people while we were waiting. He also wanted to film the unloading of all the supplies for the Lockhart Aboriginal Mission and the surrounding cattle stations. It would be quite a turn out. This boat supplied all the Aboriginal Missions and cattle stations throughout Cape York, and would only call in once a month, and during the wet season would be the only supplies they would get until the road was open.

After we set up camp we had the rest of the day to rest and clean our gear. I decided to scout the area for suitable areas to film, my wife Marcia and our daughter Lisa went with me to see what we could find. As we were driving back towards the rainforest I heard Palm Cockatoos calling off to our right about 100 meters in off the road. There was a track to the right just ahead. We turned in and drove a short distance then stopped. I said that this looks like a good spot to walk and see if we can see the cockatoos. It was open forest with pockets of rainforest along the gullies, I saw this Palm Cockatoo sitting on the entrance to a nest hollow. The tree was a Bloodwood tree about ten meters high. We sat behind a fallen dead tree and watched this cockatoo. It was calling and was holding a stick about 15 cm long (6 inches). While holding this stick it was striking the side of the nest, which made a drumming sound. Soon another cockatoo arrived and was sitting a short distance away from this bird. They began displaying to each other, whistling and calling, the bird with the stick flew over to the other bird and gave it the stick. It then flew back to the nest and started splitting the stick and dropping the twigs into the nest hollow. They appeared to be preparing this hollow for the breeding season.

As we walked further along this track the birdcalls were amazing coming from the fringe of rainforest. We heard and saw Wompoo fruit Pigeons *Ptilinopus magnificus* feeding in fig trees on the edge of the gully. These beautiful green and purple pigeons were totally unafraid of us as we got closer to them.

Another fruit pigeon that was quite common and was often seen flying overhead was the Torres-Strait Pigeon *Ducula bicolor*. This pure white pigeon with black primary wing feathers and black tail flies in flocks over the rainforest and is often seen feeding in the mangroves on the coast. Other species of birds seen that day were Blue-winged

Kookaburra *Dacelo leachii,* Forest Kingfisher *Halcyon macleayii,* Rainbow Bee-eater *Merops ornatus,* and Orange-footed Scrubfowl *Megapodius reinwardt.* These mound nesters were fairly common and we would quite often come across their huge mounds in the rainforest. Sometimes they would build these mounds of leaf mulch in the open forest as well. One nest we came across was three meters high.

On our return to camp we told Bob about the Palm Cockatoo nest we saw. He said that was what he was after and decided to film it early the next day.

The next morning the crew was up early. We loaded our gear and drove to the spot where we found the nest. There were no birds present or any to be heard either. Bob decided to set up anyway and we quickly built a hide near the nest tree and sat and waited. Palm Cockatoos, as we found out on this trip, were late risers in the morning and would not become active until the sun was well up, usually around 9 am, so we always had enough time to prepare for filming.

While we waited I heard a Red-cheeked Parrot *Geoffroyus geoffroyi* calling a short distance away. I walked closer hiding behind trees so I would not be seen. There above me was a female excavating a nest cavity. Red-cheeked Parrots and Fig Parrots are one of the few parrots that choose to excavate a nest rather than use a hollow like most of the other Australian parrots.

I could not see the male, but when I took a closer look through my binoculars I found him sitting quietly on a dead stick not far away. Through the binoculars the male had a bright red/orange face and a blue/gray crown, his overall color was light forest green, he had a deep orange beak, the female was green with a brown/gray face, and a horn coloured beak. I went back to the others and told them what I saw. Bob said we would give the Palm Cockatoos another hour and if they did not show we would move to the Red-cheeks and film them. We waited, about twenty minutes later I heard a Palm calling and it sounded like it was heading for our location. Sure enough a beautiful steely black Palm Cockatoo landed on the top of the tree above the nest hollow, its bright red cheek patch shining in the morning sunlight, its palm like crest feathers moving in the slight breeze. Cameras were rolling and we waited. Soon it flew down to the hollow and seemed to be inspecting it to see if any other bird was using it. I thought this bird was a female by her manner. She started to call and display and soon the other bird arrived, a male. He sat above her watching her inspecting the hollow. After a few minutes the hen turned and backed into the nest. I thought this strange at first, as most parrots and cockatoos enter the nest head first and then turn around once inside. She stayed inside for a few minutes then poked her head out. It made a great shot.

The female Palm Cockatoo flew up to the male and they preened each other for a while and then flew off together. Bob and Richard were very happy with the footage they shot. We moved our gear over to the Red-cheek nest and set up to film them. We made quite a bit of noise setting up and I expected the parrots to be disturbed and vacate the nest and fly away, but they took no notice of us at all, in fact we did not need to build a hide. We just set up beneath the tree and started shooting. It was incredible. Here were these rare birds, so rare that there were none in captivity here in Australia, and to my knowledge very few held overseas. We spent an hour getting the shots we wanted then returned to camp.

Next morning over breakfast I said to Bob Nelson, what are you going to do when the boat arrives tomorrow and they unload the studio van? He looked at me as if to say, "What do you mean." I said they will be unloading the truck tomorrow, and you do realize that it's too big and too high for the tracks out of here. It will not be possible to drive it back to Cairns over those rough tracks and anyway it won't make it across the Claudie River because of the muddy steep banks on either side of the river.

Bob went blank; Richard walked over to him and said Graham's right, you know, we had better talk about it and work out what we are going to do. We discussed our problem and Bob and Richard decided that when they unload the van we will drive it up here to our camp, decide what equipment we will require for our trip back south to Cairns, then get them to reload the van and return it to Cairns.

I could see that Bob was very disappointed about not having all his equipment for our return trip south. I said that none of us had ever been this far north before and at least we got here and you got the footage you were after, we should all be thankful for that.

The rest of the day was spent around camp preparing for the boat's arrival, deciding on what equipment we did not need so we could send it back in the van.

Next morning we all headed to the jetty. The boat was due in early. It would take a full day to unload the van and all the supplies for the mission, plus the supplies for the locals living at Portland Roads. This all had to be completed before the afternoon tide. Also Bob had to let them know that the van would have to go back to Cairns. Ross Pope was there at the jetty. Bob discussed the situation with him. He said providing they had time before the tide, there should not be a problem. Bob was so relieved. We all sat, watched and waited.

A short time later the boat was spotted coming around Restoration Rock, a small rocky island off Portland Roads (Restoration Rock lies just north of Restoration Island where Captain Bligh of "Mutiny of the Bounty" fame landed in 1789). The ship was much larger than I thought. By now the whole port was abuzz with all the locals. It seemed that the whole Aboriginal community of Lockhart River was there to meet this boat.

Richard and the camera crew were set up ready to film the unloading of the supplies; the rest of us sat and enjoyed the commotion. It turned out to be quite funny really; one of the locals told us that the Aboriginal community enjoyed their beer each night at the mission, where they were permitted to drink for one hour. But they had run out of beer three days ago, and this is why they were all here to help unload. They were all keen to get the beer back to the mission so they could get it cold for that night's canteen drinking session.

What they did not know was that back in Cairns all the beer and community supplies were loaded on first, which meant all the other equipment would have to be unloaded first before they could get to the beer. Everybody was very keen to help in the unloading.

Bob went and saw the Skipper of the boat to let him know that the van was to be returned to Cairns. I was watching a short distance away. I could see by the body language the Skipper was surprised to say the least. Bob returned to the film crew and continued directing.

Three hours later the unloading was completed and they told us that they wanted to load the van after they had a 30 minute break for lunch. We all returned to camp and loaded the van with the equipment we did not need for our return trip south. The van was driven to the boat and loaded, an hour later the boat sailed, suddenly the jetty was deserted and it was as if nothing had happened. The locals returned to their houses dotted along the shore. All the mission people left with their supply of beer for the next month and we returned to our camp for a late lunch and a rest.

That evening while we were all sitting around our campfire I suggested to Bob that I still wanted to try and reach the mouth of the Pascoe River, which was my original plan right from the beginning of this trip. When I first started to think about this trip two or three years earlier, all the bird books that I read all mentioned the Pascoe River. Now that we are so close, if I returned home without at least trying to get there, I know it would haunt me the rest of my life.

Bob, in his typical Yankee drawl said, "Hey boy seeing we're so close let's do it". The next morning we were heading north again along the bottom Pascoe track.

The bottom Pascoe track, as Ross Pope told us, is not a track that gets used much, in fact it's been three years since anyone had driven over it, and we would soon find out why. According to my Army survey map the distance we would have to travel was 17 miles (27km) to reach the mouth of the river. This should only take us say two to three hours, so we should be back to this camp by nightfall. The first two miles was easy going. Some of the locals must be using it looking for firewood, and we could see where they had cut timber. From that point on it became very rough and in a couple of places quite dangerous, there were many washouts and extreme care had to be taken to get the six Land Rovers through. At one point all the women bailed out of the vehicles and walked alongside because they thought the vehicles would tip over.

We were slowed down by many fallen trees that lay across our path, luckily we had a chainsaw which made life a lot easier. It was mostly open forest with patches of rainforest along the creeks that we drove through. There were plenty of Palm Cockatoos and we even found an unexpected nest that a female flew out of right alongside the track. Eclectus parrots were seen and heard as well as a few Red-cheeked parrots.

In a pocket of rainforest at a small creek where we stopped for a cup of tea, I heard some small parrots that were feeding in a large Cluster fig tree *Ficus racemosa.* They turned out to be Fig parrots *Cyclopsitta diophthalma marshalli.* This sub species called the Marshall's Fig Parrot is the smallest of the three sub species found in Australia and is identical to the Double-eyed Fig parrot *Cyclopsitta diophthalma diophthalma,* found in New Guinea. This tiny 5-inch (14cm) bird was a brilliant deep forest green, the males had bright red faces and a red crown, and the females had whitish cheek patches with a blue/gray crown. These tiny fig parrots that were not much bigger than the green unripe figs they were feeding on and were hard to distinguish among the cluster of figs, they were not afraid of our presence. We set up and filmed them and the pieces of figs that rained down on us during the filming indicated that there was a small flock of them, very little noise was being made by them until one started to call, then they all started to chatter and off they flew. At least 15 birds were counted, I hoped it looked as good on film as it did to us watching.

Our convoy was on the move again. We had only progressed about half way to the Pascoe when we entered into thick rain forest. Certainly no one had been along this track for a long time. The rainforest was starting to claim back the track that passed through it and there were many vines growing across the track that started to make our progress slow. Each time one of the vehicles got tangled in these vines it was quite a job to cut them out. One of the worst vines you can come across in the rainforest was called "Wait Awhile Vine" for if you got caught in it you had to wait awhile for someone to cut you out. It was a strong vine with what could be best described as sharp fish hooks along its length and the moment you got hooked there you would stay, because the harder you tried to get yourself free, the harder the hooks bit in. Needless to say we all soon knew what it looked like and tried to stay well clear of it.

Finally, after seven hours we reached our destination, the mouth of the Pascoe River, seven hours to travel 17 miles (27 km). If I had known it would have taken this long maybe I would have decided not to go. Anyway we were here. The width of this river surprised us all, and it was a lot wider than we expected. It looked to be close to a mile (1.6km) across, and the banks were covered in thick mangroves.

As we walked along the edge of the river we came to a grassy open area where we could see a good distance both up and down the river. While we were standing there we could smell this stench coming from a short distance away. We walked over and there in front of us was a carcass of a large crocodile. It was about 14ft. (4.2m) long. It had been shot and skinned by a croc shooter. Crocodiles were still hunted for their skins in many rivers in Australia's northern tropics, but to see them up this close had an effect on most of the crew. We could also see where other crocs had been coming ashore to feed on this carcass. It was an eerie place— you had this feeling of being watched. You could not see them but you knew they were there.

Bob had originally planned to launch our three aluminum boats and film us crossing the Pascoe; he quickly changed his mind, much to the delight of the others. We did some filming of the river then returned back along the track to set up camp for the night. It was almost dark by this time, and everyone was hungry from the long hard day.

After dinner, Bob opened a case of champagne that we had packed away just for this occasion. It was warm but what the hell! We had made it to the Pascoe River. Everybody slept well that night; no one had dreams of crocodiles in the night. The next morning we set off back to Portland Roads, it was a lot quicker coming back and took us only four hours.

We camped at the place we were a few days before. We now had to decide where we go from here. I said to Bob we should go back to the Claudie River and get some more shots of those Eclectus parrots. We also hadn't been to the airport at Iron Range or the Lockhart Aboriginal Mission. Bob agreed. Tomorrow morning we would head back inland to the rainforest.

The next morning I think all of us were keen to be on the move again. The convoy drove west up the track heading for Iron Range Airport. We were soon entering the rainforest and started to hear all those birdcalls from the array of birdlife found there. It's amazing the din these birds can make.

A mob of wild pigs ran across the road in front of us. These pigs are descendants of the ones released by Captain Cook when he beached his ship the *Endeavour* in 1770 for repairs at what is now the town of Cooktown. Wild pigs are a major pest throughout the states of New South Wales, Queensland and the Northern Territory. They do considerable damage to native vegetation, and they can also be considered dangerous if confronted while walking through the forest.

We came across wild pigs almost every day; we all soon developed into fast sprinters and tree climbers.

Our convoy stopped at a spot called Gordon's mine. This is an area that had been mined some years ago and many mine shafts are dotted about the rainforest. They mined for tin and gold and traces can still be found today. As we walked up a track leading off to the right I heard Eclectus parrots calling again. We walked for another fifteen minutes then in this tall fig tree a male started to sound the alarm. He spotted us and let out this noisy squawk, Awk! Awk! Awk! to let the female know that an intruder was below. The female stuck her head out of the nest hollow, looked at us then disappeared inside. Soon another two males joined the male sitting above the nest. They squawked and flew around a bit, then took no notice of us at all. I really found these parrots fascinating, their brilliant plumage and the amazing contrast between male and female.

As we drove further up the range closer to the airport turnoff we noticed hundreds and hundreds of rusty 44-gallon fuel drums dumped in the gullies along the track. We stopped to have a look at them and could not understand why they were dumped here. We continued on past the turnoff and headed for the airport at Iron Range. We had not traveled this way before and the surroundings were all new to us. Soon we started to drive through fenced pasture, and sighted cattle; a short distance later we came to the entrance of the cattle station called King Park.

King Park cattle station was small compared to other stations on the peninsula, but this 8,125 acre property was one of the few that were freehold and not leasehold like most of the others. As we drove in the entrance, there to our right was a world war two field artillery 25lb cannon, which at the time we thought was strange to see something like that this far north. As we pulled up near the homestead the owner came out to meet us. He introduced himself as Peter Hybis and welcomed us to King Park. Bob asked him about the 25 pounder in the driveway. Peter said they dug it out when they were clearing a section of the property. He then told us a bit of the history of Iron Range during the Second World War.

During the battle of the Pacific and later the battle of the Coral Sea, 35,000 American and Australian troops were stationed at Iron Range. The old Claudie airstrip that is a few miles south of the current Iron Range airport now lies abandoned, which explains all the rusty fuel drums in the gullies along the track. Peter Hybis told us that they could hear the fighting during the battle of the Coral Sea, and they could see the gun flashes during the night. That's how close the Japanese came to invading Australia.

Peter invited us all in for a "cuppa" and as we sat talking about this fascinating place, I asked him about the Palm Cockatoos and these beautiful Eclectus parrots that we have been filming. He said he could show us a spot where they seem to spend a lot of time. He said every time he drove through there he would see or hear them. He also said that his manager knew where there was a Palm cockatoo's nest and he would get him to show it to us. Peter came with us and we headed towards the airport. Just before we reached the airport we turned off to the right along a well used track, Peter said this was the road to the old Lockhart Mission which was about twenty miles away. After about fifteen minutes we descended down this steep hill to a concrete causeway. He said that this was part of the Claudie River. We were now entering into rainforest again. I started to hear Eclectus parrots calling, and we drove a little further then Peter told us to stop. We parked the vehicles off the road, Bob asked how much further it was and should we bring the camera gear. Peter said it was only a short walk and we should take the gear along for it might be worthwhile to film them.

We unloaded the gear and followed Peter into the rainforest. Once well inside the forest it's amazing just how easy it is to walk, there is very little undergrowth and thank God no Wait Awhile Vines. Although just before we started off Peter showed us a plant to stay well away from, it's called stinging nettle *Dendrocnide excelsa.* The underside of the plant has thousands of these fine fiber like needles that are very painful when accidentally brushed up against. He told us a funny story about a group of visitors from Cairns who were out chasing butterflies along the edge of the rainforest when one of the ladies had to go to the toilet, she darted off into the rainforest and a few minutes later this loud scream was heard. She came running out of the rainforest clutching her strides (trousers). The others thought that a Cassowary was after her, but she had used these nice green leaves to wipe herself— the leaves were from the stinging nettle plant.

Now that we knew what it looked like we would all take care to stay well away from it. Peter said it's just a little further. We must have walked at least two miles but in the end it was worth it. We came to a stand of very tall fig trees on the edge of the river. There were Eclectus parrots everywhere, their alarm calls were sounding and before we knew it there were at least eighteen of these brightly coloured parrots flying around squawking their heads off. Richard and Bob set up one camera and Bill and I set up the other. By the time we were ready to start filming all the parrots had settled down and were sitting on or close to their nest hollows, the females' heads were sticking out and I said to Bob that it would make a good shot if the camera could zoom in tight enough. He agreed and both cameras started filming.

I counted at least seven nests in the three main trees, five in the two trees across the river and two in the tree on our side of the river; we really got some great footage that day, thanks to Peter's hospitality.

Bob said by the time we get back it will be time for lunch. He invited Peter to stay and eat with us. He said that would be okay but let's have lunch at his place where we had plenty of room to park the vehicles and enjoy the shade under the Poinciana trees. We could also use the toilet and shower if we liked, much to the delight to the ladies in our crew.

After lunch we were all sitting around talking and enjoying the rest, when Bill asked Peter more about the area during the war. Peter said that there are stories that when the war was over and the troops were pulling out they bulldozed deep trenches alongside the airfield and buried tons of equipment. He said they pushed new army jeeps and Harley Davidson motor bikes into these trenches and covered them up. He said who knows what's buried under there. Peter went on to say; did we see the bombsite on the way in that morning? We said bombsite? He said yes in the 1950s they exploded a bomb containing high explosive to see what affect it had on the rainforest. It totally cleared about 500 acres. My first thoughts were "what about the wildlife." Peter said they sounded a siren just prior to the blast. I said I still bet it killed a lot of the local species.

We said our good-byes to Peter Hybis and his manager and headed for the Lockhart Aboriginal Mission which was a few miles south of King Park and the airport. Lockhart was a fairly new community having being moved from the "old site" a year or so earlier. The old Lockhart site was about 30 miles (48km) south of the new site and was hard to get to during the wet season, also there was no suitable jetty or safe landing area for supplies that had to come up from Cairns by sea.

Our convoy drove up to the community store. Bob and I walked into the office to ask for permission to enter the Aboriginal reserve (entry to any Aboriginal land or reserve has to be approved by the elders of the tribe that inhabited the area). The girl behind the counter said she would go and get one of the elders. A few minutes later she returned with an old Aboriginal man who greeted us with a big smile. We sat down on the edge of the verandah of the store and we told him what we were doing and could we purchase some supplies and fuel for our vehicles. He said we could get what supplies we wanted and also the fuel then invited us to the canteen that night for a few drinks. He said be there at seven o'clock or we could miss out.

We refueled the vehicles, purchased some supplies and decided to check out the bombsite on our way to finding a suitable campsite for the night. Now we knew what to look for it wasn't hard to find. Soon we were all standing in this huge devastated area; on first sight it looked like it had been cleared by two large bulldozers with heavy chains attached between them as nothing was left standing. Although it had been a few years since the explosion, nothing had regenerated except some ground cover and vines; again I could not help to think about the damage it must have done to the wildlife.

That night we decided to camp at a place called Reg. Cooks shack just past the turnoff to Portland Roads. Cookie's shack was deserted but often used by campers who were passing through. There was good drinking water in the rainwater tanks and not a bad place to spend the night, and it was close to the mission where we said we would go for a drink.

We had an early dinner and tidied ourselves up as best we could, some looking a lot better than others. You could see we had been in the bush too long but we did our best. Bob said we should take as few vehicles as possible, so we crammed into three Land Rovers and drove to the mission. It was dark by the time we arrived, and finding the canteen was not hard we just followed the crowd, they were all going in the same direction all carrying large glass jugs. We parked the vehicles and were greeted by the elder who met us earlier. He took us inside where we met Peter Hybis and his men from King Park; they asked us to sit down with them. The canteen was a huge open hall with a small storeroom at one end; this was where they served the beer. It was enclosed in steel mesh and the beer was passed out through a servery in the center. Peter said they had to serve the beer this way because as the evening went on, the more interesting it would become, the locals would get drunk and they would fight to get to the store for more beer. Once it started to get out of hand they would just shut the store and that would be the end of drinks for that night.

Bob asked Peter why they served the beer in jugs. Peter said because they would take cans or stubbies home or outside and pool it together and drink all night. By making them use the jugs it made them drink it all in the canteen and they could control the amount they drank.

There was a local community band playing country music and after about an hour everyone was quite merry, no fights had started and things were going well. Three of the elders came over to us and asked if we would like them to dance for us. Not quite sure what he meant we said yes, that would be great. Peter said you might like to film this, as they don't do it often for strangers. Bob said we would wait and see first. I asked Peter were they going to do a Corroboree, which was a native festive ceremonial dance. He said, well sort of but wait and see.

The store had closed as the quota of beer was now sitting in jugs on every table. It was a hot steamy night and the beer was getting warm. The dancing started, men only were allowed to dance and the women were now outside looking in through the steel mesh on the windows. Aboriginal children were running and playing on the floor. It was a sight to see. The singing and dancing got louder and louder and I saw Bob and Richard heading for the vehicles to grab the camera gear, this was not to be missed. Each dance went on for what seemed a long time. I said to Peter, this was not just Aboriginal culture, was it? He said no, it was a mix that was unique to Cape York as it was a mixture of three or four native cultures, Aboriginal, Thursday Islanders, and Solomon Islanders with a bit of Papua New Guinea thrown in as well.

I had never seen anything like this before, and would probably never see anything like it again. I glanced across to my wife and daughter, and they were tapping their feet in time with the dancers. Bob and Richard had set up and were filming the entire scene; they must have had trouble keeping the camera still as the whole building was shaking from the 30 or 40 dancers strutting their stuff. The mixture of cultures and the feeling of being as one will stay with every one of us as we gazed at these amazing dancers.

Once the dancing was over and all the beer had been drunk it was time to leave. Outside a few minor fights had started and we knew it was time to go. We said good bye to the elders and thanked them for allowing us to film them that night. We also said goodbye to Peter and his men, as we would be leaving Iron Range the next day. Bob had decided he had what he wanted as far as the Palm cockatoos and

Eclectus parrots were concerned and wanted to get back to Coen to film the races, which were on the next weekend.

Driving back to our camp I was somewhat sad to be leaving this place, there was so much to do and see. But I knew I'd be back.

Next morning we loaded up the vehicles for the rough ride west back over the range, hoping to reach the Archer River. Most of our crew I think were keen to be heading home, as it had been a long hard dusty trip and, as Bob said, we got what we came for. On the drive out my wife Marcia and I were planning to return again next year, as we both loved the place, even our daughter Lisa who was only two and a half wanted to come again too. We drove past all the places we stopped at on our way in and reached the Archer River late in the afternoon. We set up camp at the spot we had camped at a few weeks before. Still not a soul was there and we never passed any other vehicles all day.

Bob said that as this was a good place to camp we might stay a few days and drive into Coen to film the races from here each day. Coen was only an hour's drive away. We all agreed.

After a day off, we drove into Coen to see what the best time to film was. We met Mrs.Taylor again and had tea. She asked how our trip had gone and we said that we were very successful in getting the footage we wanted. The races were due to start the next day, but the best day would be the day after, Sunday, when people from all over the Cape would fly in for the day. Mrs.Taylor said that most of them would stay for the race ball that night, then fly out the next morning.

Bob and Richard discussed it and they decided that they would come in tomorrow to take some early shots of the town and the arrival of any out of town's people. I decided to stay at the Archer River camp and scout more of the river. In the end only the film crew went into town.

Next morning my wife, daughter and I set off to explore up the river. It was easy walking and every now and then we would jump in for a quick swim. There were plenty of deep pools that were formed when the river level dropped, in fact the river had dropped at least a foot since we were last here. It was early and there was plenty of wildlife about; Kangaroos were plentiful and we saw a pair of Papuan frogmouths, *Podargus papuensis,* sitting asleep in a stand of Pandanus palms. These nocturnal birds feed on large moths and flying insects at night.

Another unusual nocturnal bird we saw a lot of was the Large-tailed Nightjar *Caprimulgus macrurus.* These fascinating birds would be sitting on the track at night, and as your vehicle approached they would suddenly fly up at the last minute, and many times we would stop thinking we had hit them, then find out we never hit them at all. We had to be very careful when driving along these unused tracks because they nested on the ground— no nest, just two spotted eggs on the ground. Large-tailed Nightjars were heard every night while camping. The locals call them the "wood chopping bird" or the "donk donk bird" because of their call. It sounds like someone chopping wood some distance away "chop chop chop". We would lie in our beds at night and bet on the number of chops that it would make each time it started calling. It rarely made the same number twice and it was a great way to drift off to sleep.

Just up ahead we heard something running along the sand. We quickly gave chase; it was a trio of Scrub Turkeys or Brush Turkey, *Alectura lathami.* These ground dwellers build a mound nest similar to the Scrub fowl *Megapodius reinwardt that* were also sighted along the Archer River.

Some distance further up the river it started to open up a bit and we could now see waterfowl swimming in the shallows. We walked as quiet as we could and there just ahead of us was Australia's only member of the stork family, the Jabiru, *Ephippiorhynchus asiaticus.* This beautiful black and white stork with an iridescent green/black head and neck and bright red legs was watching for fish in the shallow water. Its reflection on the still water was a beautiful sight.

We returned to camp for lunch. Bob and Richard and the film crew had gone into town, so we had a peaceful afternoon relaxing. Late in the afternoon I went for another walk, this time down the river. It was not long before I saw another pair of Palm Cockatoos. Although they were here I was sure it was the southern limit of their range; they were not as numerous as at Iron Range, in fact I thought they were the same birds I saw on our way up weeks earlier.

It was late in the evening when the others returned from Coen. Bob said that the town was buzzing with visitors from all over the Cape. He said we would all go in early tomorrow and spend the day there. Everyone was up bright and early the next morning. We had a quick breakfast and headed for town. Bob was right— the town was alive with people, it was even hard to find somewhere to park our vehicles. There were tents set up in the main street (there is only one street) one or two caravans and plenty of people camping in the back of their Ute's (pick-up trucks) lined both sides of the street.

The racecourse was just a short walk behind the town. After each race everybody would head back to the pub for a beer. Everyone was so friendly and it turned out to be a great day. After the last race the pub was the only place to be. It spilled out into the street; people set up tables and chairs and just sat anywhere they could find a spot. The odd fight broke out but was soon defused by the two policemen stationed in the town. After nightfall all the town lights came on, plus the many coloured lights put up for the occasion. It was quite a sight, a sight I did not expect to see this far north.

The race ball had started. We were all invited to attend, and we decided we needed something to eat as we all missed out on lunch due to the filming. We arranged for some hamburgers and tea and found a place to sit. After tea Bob and the crew went to the ball to get some shots of the dancing, while the rest of us just sat and enjoyed each other's company. Later we walked over to the ball and watched everybody having a good time; there were certainly some sights to see. It was one am by the time we reached our camp at the Archer River.

We slept late the next morning; nobody stirred until Hans was heard stoking the ashes of the fire of the night before. Soon all were awake. Few had hangovers from the night before, but a good breakfast soon perked everyone up. After breakfast Bob told us he wanted to head back to Cairns, as that was the next place he wanted to film to complete his documentary of this trip. We all went quiet for a while, but soon realized he was right. We started to pack our gear for the long trip home.

Within the hour we were loaded and heading south. We had a short stop at Coen for fuel and to say goodbye to all our new friends we had met there the night before. We all thanked Mrs.Taylor for all her help and I said I hoped to see her again next year.

We had one more night camping out before we reached Cairns two days later; we headed straight for Ellis Beach and set up where we camped on our way up. There were more tourists staying at the Caravan Park— it was popular because it was right on the beach. Bob said we would stay a few days to film in and around Cairns and out on the Barrier Reef. He also had to see if the studio van had arrived back in port.

The next day Bob and the crew went into Cairns to check on the van and to do some filming of the city. My wife, daughter and I decided to drive around and get to know the area a bit. We were discussing privately that we were thinking of Cairns as a suitable place to develop a bird park. We had visited Cairns three years earlier on holiday with my parents.

Land around Ellis Beach was cheap compared to Sydney prices, and although it was 14 miles (22km) north of Cairns, it was the tourist drive north to Port Douglas and Mossman. We drove around looking at suitable sites and called into a couple of Real Estate agents to get information on current land prices. On the long drive back to Sydney we would have plenty of time to think about our future.

Over the next three days we filmed in and around Cairns and spent a day at Green Island filming the Great Barrier Reef. This small low wooded island lies 16 miles (25km) due east of Cairns; it's a great place to spend the day, with plenty of snorkeling around the coral reefs there. It was a great way to end our expedition to Cape York.

The van had arrived during those three days. Bob spent the last afternoon checking that everything was there and we prepared to leave early the next morning.

Our return trip south to Sydney would be via the Bruce Highway and the Pacific Highway down the East Coast. The return trip would take four days. We all had time to reflect on the past eight weeks, I for one could not stop thinking about those beautiful Eclectus Parrots of Iron Range.

once we were sure that they were nesting we would then decide if it was a safe tree to climb. These giant fig trees have huge buttresses with wall like roots growing out from the base of the tree, standing beside one of these walls you could not see over the top to the other side; this tree was at least 120 feet (36.5m) high. The bark was smooth and climbing would be difficult. We each chose a position at the base of the tree so that we could see a section of the tree above. Our plan was to tap the tree and observe where any female poked her head out to see what was going on. I tapped: right away the Metallic Starlings flew off in one large flock. This created quite a din. But no Eclectus parrots were seen. I tapped again, this time a lot harder, the tree echoed like a drum, one female Eclectus parrot flew out squawking and two others were sighted sticking their heads out. No wonder this tree had metal spikes driven in it. Soon we had quite a large flock of Eclectus Parrots circling us; at least a dozen birds were counted.

We returned to camp, had dinner and then sat around the campfire and planned how we would climb this giant of the forest. Our tree climbing equipment was not the modern climbing gear of today; it was basic but safe. It consisted of a 100ft. (30m) steel rope ladder, 200ft. (60m) nylon climbing rope, 500ft. (152m) of 60lb.fishing line and lead sinkers of various weights and sizes, and the most important piece of equipment a purpose built "shanghai"or slingshot. The shanghai was made of welded ½" steel rod with an arm brace, the rubbers were of speargun rubber that was so strong, it could shoot a one ounce sinker out of sight if you fired it into the air.

Next morning we carried the tree climbing gear to the base of the tree and prepared to set up. Oskar was the climber and I was the shooter. We selected a strong branch close to one of the nesting hollows. Ray and I went out onto the track to see if we had a clear shot over this branch. This tree was so straight and tall the first branches were 60ft. (18m) from the ground. Ray's job was to hold the spool containing the fishing line and point it towards the branch I was aiming for. Sounds easy, but if it's not placed just right it becomes a problem for the climber. My first shot was a shocker! The line got tangled as it left the spool; my second shot missed the branch by ten feet. The third try hit its mark and the lead was over. The next problem was to get the sinker to reach the ground on the other side of the tree. Because we were in rainforest there was plenty of scrub around this tree, and we could not locate the sinker. I decided to pull the line back a bit to see if we could locate it. Oskar spotted it in the leaves of the tree behind. He said to pull it back slowly. I did and the sinker came out without getting tangled. I lowered it to the ground.

As Oskar was the climber it was his job to tie the Nylon climbing rope to the steel rope ladder, this way the climber would be more confident knowing he tied the knots. Once we pulled the Nylon rope over we all gave a hand to pull the ladder up. I always like to pull the first two rungs of the ladder over the branch we are climbing; this helps to stop sag and also helps to stop the ladder spinning while you are climbing. By the time we did this, the bottom of the ladder was ten feet above the ground; this meant Oskar was doing a climb of over 110ft. (33.5m). And we would have to tie a rope to the bottom of the ladder so Ray and I could anchor it.

While Oskar was getting ready to make the climb, Ray and I tested the ladder by supporting our weight on the anchor rope. If it held the both of us it would certainly support Oskar. The first climb on a trip such as this was the most difficult and we possibly chose the most difficult tree in the forest to climb first. Also extra care had to be taken because of where we were. If we had an accident the closest medical treatment was 30 miles (48km) away at Lockhart Aboriginal Community, and if it were a more serious fall then they would have to be flown back to Cairns.

Oskar was ready to climb. I ran through the details of what information I wanted if it turned out to be an active nest. This was not Oskar's first climb on this ladder— we had used it many times in the past. Up he went, climbing not as you would a normal ladder, but up one side, hand over hand and one foot after the other. Climbing the ladder this way helped to stop the ladder from turning. While climbing the rest of us would be very quiet, for any distraction may break his concentration. We would watch and wait, until he left the ladder and sat on the branch to catch his breath.

After a few minutes he would signal or call out that he was okay, then he would try and reach the nest hollow to check on nest activity. "Two eggs," he called out. Then he returned to the ladder. It was important not to take too long as the hen could desert the nest. As he descended the ladder he called out that there was another nest in the main trunk of the tree about 20ft (6m) below the nest he just checked, but the ladder was at least 10ft. (3.4m) away from the tree. He said we would have to pull him closer. He held on while we tried to pull him closer to the tree. After two attempts he managed to grab a hold of the nest cavity and have a look in, just scratching, he called out and descended down the ladder. After he had rested, I asked him if there was a third nest. He said there was but we would have to re shoot the line over because it was further up and out on a higher branch. I decided we would watch late that afternoon and see if this nest was being used, also we could check if the other females returned to their nests. We lowered the climbing gear, packed up and returned to camp. Over a cup of tea Oskar gave me the details for my diary. Height of nest— approx.115ft. (44m) above the ground; depth of nest cavity —3ft. (900mm); nesting material— wood dust, chewed leaves and moist; size of entrance to the nest —approx. 6" (152mm). Two white freshly laid eggs, other comments— Oskar said it was his opinion that this nest was used every season due to the amount of feathers and scratching of the material in the bottom of the nest. He said the second nest was a lot wetter than the one that had the two eggs in it and the pair were just scratching, maybe helping to dry it out. He said this nest was not as deep, as he could touch the bottom without stretching. It was a tight fit but was a suitable nest.

After lunch we decided to drive past the airport turnoff and drive down to the top Pascoe track. This was the area where we saw plenty of activity last year. We heard and saw Palm Cockatoos. I remembered that there was a nest tree that I found last year that a pair of Palms were working, so it was worth a check. As we approached this tree a female Palm Cockatoo flew out. We decided to carry the tree climbing gear in and climb it. The tree was a eucalyptus species about 40ft. (12m.) high, and would be an easy climb. Within a few minutes we had the ladder up and Oskar was peering inside the nest. "One egg," he called out. He came down and both Ray and I climbed up to have a look at our first Palm Cockatoo nest. This tree I dubbed the "69 Tree" and noted the details in my diary.

Ray and Oskar wanted to photograph the nest and the egg in the nest, so up he went again. We then lowered the gear and decided to build a hide so we could photograph the Palms when they returned. This only took a few minutes. We placed branches up against a tree about 30ft. (9m) away from the nesting tree. I moved the vehicle out of sight and returned to the hide. Ray and Oskar had their cameras set up on tripods and were ready. I was still trying to get set up when we heard them calling a short distance away. Both birds landed in the uppermost branches above the nest, where they began bowing and displaying. The female was looking at the nest to see if it had been disturbed. Within a minute or two she flew down to the top of the hollow, looked in, saw everything was all right, then turned around and backed into the nest. All this time the male Palm Cockatoo was sitting and preening himself.

We took many great photos; they are truly magnificent looking cockatoos, the bright red cheek patch and the steel blue/black feathers were a wonderful contrast against the backdrop of the rich green forest. We decided that I would walk away from the hide so the male would see me: he would alert the hen and Ray and Oskar could get a shot of the female leaving the nest. This worked well and a series of photos of the female sitting and then flying off the entrance to the nest were taken.

Driving further along the top Pascoe track we came across a flock of Sulphur-crested Cockatoos *Cacatua galerita* feeding on fallen Pandanus nuts *Pandanus spiralis*. We stopped and I asked Ray (who I believed was possibly the best cockatoo man in the country,) what sub species he thought they were. I told him of my observations that I made last year that I thought they were smaller than *Cacatua galerita* and had a different call. Ray watched them through his binoculars for some time. (Ray was a licensed trapper of cockatoos and has handled thousands of birds over the years. White cockatoos are an unprotected species in most states of Australia, and do untold damage to crops.) He said, you are right, they are a lot different than the ones I trapped down south.

As we approached them they flew off to some nearby trees screeching loudly. Ray said they certainly have a different call, we should see if we can locate a nest to see if we can gather some information on their nesting habits, then we can compare them with the southern sub species.

We ventured further along the track until we reached the place where I saw Eclectus parrots last year. All was quite. We walked in towards the nest tree along the dry creek bed. There were a few fresh water pools here and there and keeping our progress quiet was difficult, due to the dry fallen pandanus palm fronds that lay in the creek bed. Suddenly, "Ark! Ark! Ark!" as a female Eclectus flew out of a hollow. The scrub was too thick to see either the bird or which hollow she flew from. When we all reached the tree we could see that this tree had up to three suitable nest hollows.

Deciding to climb this tree Oskar and I returned back to the vehicle to collect the climbing gear. Ray, Jan and my wife and daughter stayed at the nest in case the female returned so they could see which hollow she entered. Twenty minutes later we were back at the tree. Ray said the female did come back but saw them and was now sitting in a tree a short distance away. We quickly raised the ladder, this tree was not that high, and I managed to get the sinker and line over first try. Soon

Oskar was at the first nest, "just scratching" he called out, this meant that the nest was being worked and eggs would be laid shortly. He climbed further up the tree to the next hollow, "one egg" he called out. I called back to him "is it fresh laid?" Oskar called out "yes".

There was one more hollow left to check, but he had to move the ladder first, and this took a few minutes. He climbed up to the highest nesting hollow and was looking in. He called out "it's to dark, I will need my torch". He reached into his kit bag he carried around his neck and took out his torch. He looked in again: "two chicks about five days old". He descended the ladder and we packed up and left the area so the female could return to her chicks.

On returning to the vehicle Oskar gave me the details on each nest for my diary. Nest (1) just scratching, fresh nesting material plus some green gum leaves. When females start to prepare a hollow to nest in, they first spend a lot of time scratching up all the old nesting material from last year or the previous nest this season. They also chew on the inside of the nest hollow. This helps to add fresh material for her nest, it also starts her ovulating and constant mating with the male. Depth of nest, about 2ft.6 inches (760mm), first inch of material dry, the remainder moist. The type of tree Bloodwood, *Eucalyptus polycarpa,* nest height from ground 28ft. (8.5m). Nest entrance size approx.7" (177mm).

Nest (2) one egg fresh laid. Depth of nest 3ft. (900mm), nesting material fine wood dust and small pieces of chewed wood, dry and a little moist. Nest height from ground 35ft. (10.6m), nest entrance size approx. 6" (152mm).

Nest (3) Two chicks about five days old, depth of nest (this was the deepest found so far) approx. 5ft. (1.5m), very dark hard to see chicks without torch, chicks naked, eyes not open, cracked eggshell to one side. Nesting material? Could not reach. Nest height from ground 42ft. (12.8m), nest entrance size approx. 6" (152mm).

After waiting about half an hour Oskar went back to the nest tree to check if the females had returned. We were to start the vehicle up and drive a short distance up the track to see if the noise would make the females put their heads out. Oskar returned to the vehicle a short time later saying that he saw two hens at their nests, the one with the two chicks and the one that had the egg. We were very happy with the information collected that day, and returned to camp.

The next day we decided to drive down to Portland Roads, spend the morning at the jetty and beach, and call into see the Popes, then check the bottom Pascoe track on our way back. On our way there, as we were passing through the Gordon Mine area, I heard Eclectus calling off to our left. This area is thick rainforest with creeks and steep gullies. We parked the vehicles off the track and started walking along the edge of the creek. We had not gone far when we heard the fluted call of a female at nest. Moments later we heard a male calling as he approached the tree where we thought the female was nesting. He landed but we could not see exactly where. We crept closer, our eyes focused on the trees above. Suddenly the male flew off squawking loudly; he had seen us.

We knew what tree they were in but could not locate the nest. I told Oskar to clap his hands a few times, and out popped this bright red head of an Eclectus parrot. The tree was a very large ficus tree, the same species as the spike tree; they seemed to have a preference for these trees. Was it because they are usually the tallest trees in the rainforest? Or was it because they always seemed to have suitable nesting hollows. A bit of both, I would expect. We decided to check it again on our way back from the port. On our way back to the vehicles Oskar spotted a Marshall's Fig Parrot *Cyclopsitta diophthalma marshalli* excavating a nest high in a decaying branch of a eucalyptus tree. He only noticed it by the falling wood dust kicked out of the cavity by this tiny parrot. What was also unusual about this nest was its position on the underside of the branch. Most other parrots choose to nest in a spout or hollow on the upper side of the tree to allow easy access and sunlight to enter the nest. This nest was tucked away in the bend of the branch in complete shade. If Oskar had not seen the wood dust falling, we would never have known it was there.

I noted in my diary the position of the Eclectus parrot's nest and noted remarks about the fig parrot. I also noted that I would like to spend more time here before we leave.

We arrived at the port, and the tide was in so we decided to do some fishing off the end of the jetty, Oskar went looking for oysters on the rocks. We fished for about an hour and caught some nice fish for that night's meal; it would be a good change from what we had been used too. Oskar got a swag of black lip oysters. These oysters were the largest I'd ever seen, and were the size of your hand. One of these would equal four normal size oysters. We drove the short distance to the Pope's house; it was good to catch up with them again. They asked how the trip last year finished up. I said it was a great trip from my point of view, it was a great experience for my family, and it also convinced us to come again this year as we were thinking of moving up to Cairns to live, which would give us the opportunity of making regular trips to Iron Range.

They invited us for a cup of tea; we stayed for an hour or so then headed back to the bottom Pascoe track. This track did not impress me as much as the top track did, it was closer to the coast and mangrove swamps and contained little rainforest. It was good for Palm Cockatoos and birds of the open forest. We drove in a few miles then decided to leave the vehicles for a while and walk. We soon heard Palm Cockatoos calling ahead of us. As we walked along this track we spotted a Red-cheeked parrot *Geoffriyus geoffroyi* calling in a tree on the edge of the track. We stopped and were looking through our binoculars. We soon found the nest; the female who has a brown head was poking her head out to see what the male was squawking about.

These parrots excavate a nest cavity similar to the Fig parrots, usually in a decaying branch pointing vertically into the air. They excavate a short tunnel leading to a dome shaped cavity, where they usually lay three eggs. This is one species I would like to work on in the future. Further along this track we saw a group of Palm Cockatoos sunbathing and preening themselves in the midday sun. Oskar disappeared into the bush to our left. Later he called us over; he found another Palm Cockatoos' nest. This nest was so low we could just boost Oskar up onto my shoulders and he pulled himself up another few feet to see into the nest. "Fresh sticks" he called out. Palm cockatoos spend months leading up to the breeding season collecting twigs, flying to a number of nesting trees and then splitting these twigs into strips and dropping them into the nest. This helps to prevent water logging during heavy rains. Some nests we found on this trip had up to six feet (1.8m) of twigs, which would indicate to me that these nests were used each season by Palm cockatoos. It could even be the same pair.

We only traveled as far as the thick vine area we had to clear before driving through last year. It's amazing how quickly the scrub has grown back, no one had been through this year. We decided to return to camp. It was mid afternoon by the time we got back, so we had a late lunch and remained in camp for the rest of the day.

Next morning, after a dinner of fresh grilled fish and oysters cooked in their shells, we were all a little lazy and did not stir too early; everyone was waiting for someone else to make the first move. Soon Oskar was breaking sticks for the fire; soon we were all up ready to tackle the day.

Over a light breakfast we planned out the rest of the day. I said I would like to climb a few more Eclectus nests to gather a bit more information, and suggested that we drive to King Park station to see Peter Hybis and his men, then go to the causeway, along the road to the old Lockhart Aboriginal mission. The others agreed, and soon we were at King Park station. Peter was away in Cairns and the new manager Graham Burst greeted us. Not much had changed since we were here last year.

After a short stay at King Park we headed across the end of the airstrip towards the causeway that lay across the Claudie River. This area was very interesting to me last year because we saw many Eclectus along this section of the river. I wanted to show the others the nesting trees that had quite a number of nests in them; this is where we saw the most number of these beautiful birds. Oskar and I shared the carrying of the ladder bag for the two-mile hike down the river. A hundred foot of steel rope ladder plus two hundred feet of climbing rope was like carrying a sack of potatoes on your back, plus the heat and humidity. Needless to say we had quite a few rest periods along the way.

About halfway to the nesting trees, we were walking in dense rainforest— you could not see the sun or the sky above you; the undergrowth was easy to walk through. Suddenly Oskar stopped, he signaled to Ray and me to join him, which we did. He said someone was mist netting here and pointed to a mist net hanging in the trees ahead of us. Ray, who was an experienced trapper, inspected the net. He said it's been here for a while, a couple of weeks at least. He supposed someone set it here and then could not find it when they came back to inspect it. We carefully took it down; thankfully there was only one small dead bird in the net.

We continued onto our nest site, discussing as we went the possibility of the species they were after. Ray said that it might have been someone from the museum collecting specimens for identification of a certain species found only in this area. This sounded logical to us and we soon forgot all about it.

We started hearing Eclectus parrots calling as we approached the nesting trees. We dropped the tree climbing gear and crept in for a closer look. There was a huge fig tree across the river. It sounded like there were plenty of pairs nesting. We decided to sit and watch them for a while and try and see which hollows they were using. After about thirty minutes and cameras ready I clapped my hands. Oh what a noise they made, it sounded like twenty birds or more. As they settled down we counted three nests in the tree across the river, and there were more pairs nesting further down the river. There were at least eight pairs flying around us.

On deciding to climb the tree across the river, we first had to find a way across the Claudie. About a hundred yards back up the river a giant of the forest had fallen and it was our away across. I helped Oskar with the ladder up onto his shoulders and said don't fall in as there are big saltwater crocodiles in here. He said thanks for the encouragement. He made it across okay; the rest of us followed, although the ladies decided to stay on the other side, where they could watch the fun. This tree was high, about 140ft. (42.5m). It was going to take a good shot to get the lead sinker over. Surprisingly my first attempt went straight between the two limbs that I was aiming for. Twenty minutes later Oskar was ready to climb.

The noise these parrots made was deafening, Oskar made it to the first nest, but with all the noise we could not hear what he was saying. The male Eclectus parrots were flying quite close to him, screeching almost in his ears. He proceeded further up the ladder to the second nest, looked in, then tried to see if he could reach the third nest, but then he started to climb down to the ground. After he caught his breath he described each of the two nests he managed to inspect. He said the third nest would need another shot and we would have to move the ladder, also the end of the ladder would be off the ground by at least fifteen feet, which could be dangerous if we could not anchor it securely. I decided that we had the information from two of the nests and it did not warrant a risky climb to reach the third nest.

Oskar gave me the details of the first nest, (1) Two dark eggs, of approximately twenty days incubation. Depth of nest, three feet (900mm). Nesting material, moist wood dust, leaves and feathers. Type of tree, large ficus. Height from ground, 75ft. (22.8m). Size of nest entrance, five inches (127mm).

Nest (2) Two fairly fresh eggs, could be six to seven days incubation. Depth of nest, at least four feet, and possibly five feet (1.5 m) (could just see the eggs). Nesting material, hard to tell but appeared much the same as nest one. Height from the ground, 82ft. (24.9m). Size of nest entrance, approx. six inches (152mm).

Oskar said there was a third pair of Eclectus occupying the third and highest nest. He saw the female enter the nest while he was climbing up the ladder. He estimated the height of that nest around 100ft. (30.48m) from the ground. This is now the second tree that has contained three active nests. Is it just because it's been a good breeding season, or could it be because there are limited nest sites, or a limited number of these huge fig trees in the rainforest? This is something I would like to know, and I hoped I would get the chance to find out in the years to come.

We packed up the gear and made the long walk back to the vehicles. It was the middle of the afternoon by the time we reached our camp at the Claudie; we had a late lunch and rested the rest of the day. Here in the tropical rainforest you have to pace yourself because of the heat and high humidity. The best times of the day are early morning and late in the afternoon. During the heat around midday we would try and do as little as possible, unless of course we were climbing, as we were this morning. This is when it's very exciting and we tend to lose track of time.

Time was running short. The others had to return south and my wife and I wanted a couple of days in Cairns to look around. After dinner that night we discussed what we had to do before we left. I said I had two more areas that I would like to check before we headed south. These were Wymouth cattle station and Lamond Hill; both these areas could be checked in a day if we started early. We all agreed to make an early start the next morning, check the two remaining areas and then pack up camp and head south the following day.

At daylight the next morning everyone was up early. After breakfast we headed down towards Portland Roads again. This time we would be only going about halfway to the port, a distance of about twenty miles (32km). Wymouth cattle station was very run down. The old homestead was deserted. We looked around but could not see anyone. We decided to drive in across the open cattle paddocks to a section of rainforest I saw last year. I noticed a lot of Eclectus parrots heading over that way; I wanted to have a closer look.

For all the time we have been observing these parrots we had not seen them feeding in any particular area or feeding in groups. I needed information on their daily feeding habits, and this could be that area.

We parked the two Land Rovers under a large shade tree and walked along the edge of the rainforest. Armed with only our binoculars and cameras we walked a mile or so when I spotted a small group of Eclectus parrots flying across the open forest towards us. We hid behind the trees and they landed about a hundred feet ahead of us. I said to the others to wait a few minutes to let them settle and then we could quietly approach them. Oskar decided to head off to the left and try and get on the other side of them. We crept closer to them. They were just on the fringe of the rainforest feeding on a tree that had small thumbnail size fruits. Through my binoculars I thought they looked like "Nonda Plums" *Parinari nonda* which was a favorite fruit of the Palm Cockatoos.

Off to the left of these birds there was a single male sitting in a tree feeding on the blossom of the "Cocky apple" *Planchonia careya* tree. These rough bark trees are also called bush mango and wild quince trees. After the parrots flew off we collected some fallen fruits and blossoms from beneath the trees. These I would take back with me for proper identification back in Cairns. Going on the amount of half eaten fruit that lay on the ground below these trees, and the fallen blossoms, we had to assume that this was a popular feeding area for these parrots.

Oskar returned with a handful of wild plums he had found under a tree further along the edge of the rainforest. We followed him back to the spot where he found them. They looked like Burdekin plums *Pleiogynium timorense* to me, and these were partly eaten too. One of the locals down at the port told us that there was a species of plum that they called the Wongi plum *Manilkara kauki*— was this them? Walking back to our vehicles we decided to cross to the other side of this strip of rainforest, expecting to come across a creek in the middle of this patch of scrub. There was no creek, just rainforest where cattle had grazed; it was a nice easy walk. Before we returned to the vehicles we found another area where birds had been feeding earlier that morning. I collected some more fruits from a Nonda plum tree. Judging by the black feathers we found on the ground Palm cockatoos were feeding here as well.

We left the deserted Wymouth cattle station and drove back towards the Iron Range airport. Lamond Hill lies to the east as we drove towards the airport. This large hill is covered in mostly thick open forest with only its peak covered in rainforest. I noticed this hill last year but never had a chance to survey it for possible nesting sites. It's one of those areas that you think to yourself, "If I was a bird this is where I would be" type of places. I found a track leading off to the left, it was almost overgrown with high guinea grass but once in off the main track it was fairly easy going. We parked the two Land Rovers just off the track and proceeded to walk the area. It wasn't too long before we heard Palm cockatoos calling over to our left. We decided to investigate. Oskar was in the lead, suddenly he disappeared from sight! He had fallen into what turned out to be a Second World War slit trench. Here we were walking through chest high guinea grass and he falls into a ditch.

Oskar was unhurt. It turned out to be quite funny really. We made him pay for his disappearing act the rest of the day, he being German and all. We ribbed him about the war and he had to come to Australia to fall into one of our trenches.

It turned out that this whole area around Lamond Hill was fortified during the war. Later when we reached the top of this hill we could see why. We had a 360-degree view of the surrounding area; we could see the coast, both north and south for miles. The top of this hill had been cleared during the war, but the rainforest was slowly claiming it back. There were sections of concrete lying scattered in the forest. We thought it was possibly a gun emplacement for the impending Japanese invasion of Australia, which thankfully did not take place.

Walking through this area we had to be very careful. It would have been disastrous if we had decided to drive the vehicles in. That day we found three active Palm cockatoos *Probosciger aterrimus macgillivrayi* nests, one Marshall's fig parrots *Cyclopsitta diophthalma marshalli* nest and a Red-cheeked parrots *Geoffroyus geoffroyi* nest, but no Eclectus parrots *Eclectus roratus macgillivrayi* nests.

We returned to camp, had another late lunch then started packing up our gear. I brought my diary up to date before taking a last walk late in the day to the spike tree for one last look at these magnificent red and green parrots. As I stood there leaning up against one of these giant rainforest trees peering through my binoculars at these beautiful birds, I thought quietly to myself "someday I will come back".

The dusty three-day drive back south to Cairns was uneventful; we camped at the Hann and Laura rivers and sighted plenty of wildlife. But the moment we hit the bitumen and we started seeing civilization again, quietly in my thoughts I was planning our return to the wilds of Cape York.

Little did I know then it would be five years before Oskar and I were again heading for the Cape.

The few days my family and I spent in Cairns at the end of the 1969 trip went a long way to helping us make up our minds about starting this new life living in the far north. We knew that once we returned to Sydney, the cold winter and the rat race were not for us.

Two years later my family and I packed up and moved to sunny north Queensland to start a bird park. In June 1972, after six busy months of planning and construction we opened the bird park to the public. All my birds that I had in Sydney arrived a few days before the opening day and were released into their new flights. It was a great feeling to finally have them housed in family groups, one pair per aviary. My basic plan was a simple one; there were 52 species of Australian Parrots and Cockatoos. So I built 52 breeding aviaries hoping to some day display them all, something that has not been achieved to this day, by any Zoo or bird park. Species that I could not obtain from other Zoos, bird parks or from private bird breeders, I would collect from the wild on permit.

I had to wait until 1975 before the wildlife authorities would grant me a license to collect (new Bird Park proprietors were required to operate for three years before collecting permits were even considered). This I thought was fair enough, I needed time to get the park established and plan what I would like to collect first.

Oskar had finished working at Exmouth Gulf in Western Australia, and was now working at the bauxite mining town of Weipa. Weipa is in Cape York due west of Iron Range. In October 1974 Oskar and I did a short scouting trip to Iron Range to check if the nesting sites we had found in 1968 and 1969 were still active. Also we hoped to locate some new ones, and prepare a list of species I wanted to collect next year (1975).

Most of the nests were being used. My plan of going later in the season was a good one; the Eclectus nests we climbed all had half grown chicks in them and the two Palm cockatoo nests we inspected had fully feathered young inside. We hoped the following year would be as good.

In January 1975 I applied for our first collecting permit. I listed the species and number of what we wanted to collect, four Palm cockatoos *Probosciger aterrimus macgillivrayi*. Four Eclectus parrots *Eclectus roratus macgillivrayi*. Four Red-cheeked parrots *Geoffroyus geoffroyi*. And four Fig parrots *Cyclopsitta diophthalma marshalli*.

Of the four species only the Palm cockatoo was in captivity at Taronga Zoo in Sydney, but these were the New Guinea sub species *Probosciger aterrimus*. My plan was to collect only young from the nest. This way they could adapt better to captivity and be quieter for the public. As a breeder I had a lot of experience with hand feeding so to me this was my preferred way to collect these birds. This method of collecting also had little impact on the wild population as no adult or bonded birds would be taken.

Living in far north Queensland the main tourist season was during the dry season. It would start in April, at Easter and go through to the end of October. From the end of October until the end of March it was the wet season; storms would start late November through December and the real wet would be during the months of January, February and March.

During the real wet, February and March, there is not a lot to do. There were no tourists and some days we would open the park and not get one visitor through the whole day. My neighbor Gunter Gertz, who was an artist and signwriter and did all the signs for our bird park, suggested that we do a trip to Iron Range by air to see what the birds did during the wet season. I thought this was a great idea. Gunter wanted to do some paintings of the rainforest and I could check to see if any nesting was going on.

On the 5th of February we took the short one hour flight from Cairns. In those days the flight was with Bush Pilot Airways in an old DC-3 aircraft. It was a real experience. The locals called them "Goony Birds." I had arranged to be met at Iron Range by the family who looked after the airport. They kindly loaned us two pushbikes to ride around on. They were also kind enough to have one of the ground staff drive us to Reg Cooks Shack, along the Portland Roads track.

I chose this spot because in was in the center of the areas we had worked in 1968 and 1969, and because we only had pushbikes to get around. We would be able to cover a wider area in either direction. It was also the wet season, and we would at least have some shelter from the daily downpour of rain.

Reg Cooks Shack is just that; in fact describing it as a shack may be too kind.

Reg Cooks Shack or Cookies Shack as the locals called it was a collection of rusting sheets of corrugated iron, just off the road at the edge of the rainforest. It was a roof and four walls and a verandah, there were no doors and the windows were just openings or a push out shutter. Inside it looked like wild pigs had been using it to dust bath in the earth floor, but it was dry.

After a bit of house cleaning it was suitable to camp in for the short time we were there. Ron who drove us there said he would come after work and drive us to check some of our nest trees. Gunter and I decided to take the pushbikes and spend the day looking for our nests to see if there was activity. We spent about three hours looking at some of our nests and looking for new ones, of which we found three. This meant we had eight nests to check the following day. Ron arrived at four in the afternoon. We decided to head west out along the Coen road to see if we could reach the "Spike Tree." The vehicle only made it as far as the first crossing of the Claudie River. A large tree had fallen during the last storm and was blocking the track; we left the vehicle and decided to walk the rest of the way. The height of the river was about three feet (900mm) and flowing fast. We stripped off and waded across holding our clothes above our heads. On reaching the other side we slipped and slid our way up the muddy bank. Got dressed and walked to the middle crossing of the Claudie River. All this time we did not hear any Eclectus parrots calling.

I said to the others that I would cross and they could stay on this side, no sense in all of us getting wet. I stripped off again and crossed the river. It was a little deeper than the first crossing, and it must have been raining further up stream. I made it to the other side okay but had a fright about half way across. Something brushed against my leg and my first thought was "Croc." It turned out to be a large scrub python, but it certainly raised the hairs on the back of my neck. The "Spike Tree" was deserted; even all the Starlings nests were hanging untidily in the wind, and most had already fallen to the ground. As I was walking back a small group of Eclectus parrots flew overhead.

I crossed back over the river and rejoined the others. As we drove slowly back towards camp I saw a Palm cockatoo fly off from a hollow to our left. It wasn't one of our known trees so we decided to investigate. The tree was only about 15ft. (4.5m) high and the wooden extension ladder Ron had would be long enough to reach it; I climbed up, no chick or egg! But it was an active nest. I estimated the depth of the platform of sticks to be about three feet (900mm) deep, there were some fresh looking sticks and a few dry green gum leaves. The depth from the top of the hollow to the platform was only 2ft.6 inches (762 mm), so not very deep. I noted the position of this nest on my map and entered it in my diary. We returned to camp.

Ron stayed for a cup of tea and said he would be able to come and pick us up the next morning if we liked, as it was his day off and it would give him something to do. We said that would be great, he said goodbye, and he would see us in the morning at about 9.30am.

Just as it got dark that night it started to rain. Over the next few hours it became heavier, until it was torrential. The roof above our sleeping bags was starting to leak, but luckily for us I packed an extra sheet of plastic, and we covered ourselves up and hoped for the best. We did not get much sleep that night. It blew a gale for about three hours plus we had some unexpected visitors during the night. I got up to check if the bikes and some of our gear was under shelter, and because we did not have a door to close I just had a sheet of corrugated iron laying across the opening. Although I had a flashlight I proceeded to step over this sheet of iron, when something didn't feel right. I shone the flashlight to where I was about to step and there was a huge scrub python slithering along the top edge of the sheet of iron. I called out to Gunter to come and have a look at it. He swore something in German and came over to have a closer look, and this snake was at least 16ft. (4.8m) long and would have been at least eight inches (203mm) thick. I gave it a nudge and sent it on its way.

A couple of wild pigs decided to shelter from the storm during the night, but they too left us once they got scent of us there. The next morning the rain had stopped, but everywhere was flooded. We took our camping gear outside to dry in the sun. After the very wet night we did not expect Ron to turn up, but at 9. 30 he arrived. After a cup of tea we loaded the climbing gear in the back of the Land Rover and headed down towards the port and the top Pascoe track.

Using the wooden extension ladder we checked all the low Palm cockatoo nests fairly quickly in the east pocket on the right hand side of the track. The four nests we climbed all were used this breeding season. They were all soiled and two of them contained bits of egg shell, so I assume the chicks hatched and the young had fledged. It was disappointing not to find any fully feathered chicks in any of these nests. The last tree we climbed was the 69 tree but again we were too late, the chick had flown.

We returned to camp, a soaking wet and disappointed lot; we had lunch and said goodbye to Ron. It rained the rest of the afternoon so we stayed in the shack and tried to dry out our clothes. Gunter did some sketching and I went over my notes.

That night we heard on the radio that the night before when it poured, a low-pressure trough had passed over us, and 15inches (381mm) of rain was recorded at the airport at Iron Range. A cyclone had just missed us.

The next day was a beautiful morning, there wasn't a cloud in the sky. Gunter called out to me that he could hear Eclectus parrots calling in the rainforest. We went to investigate when we heard a truck coming, so we returned to the shack. It was Eddie, one of the men who worked at the airport. He decided to come out and see if we wanted a hand. I asked him if he knew of any areas where Eclectus parrots or Palm cockatoos fed or congregated. He said that there was an area near the old airport that he had seen Palms feeding on Pandanus fruit. I said could you take us there. No problem, he said.

The truck was a two tonner with dual wheels at the rear so we hoped it would not get bogged. We loaded our gear and off we went. The area he had taken us was new to me and I was excited about finding something new. Eddie told us something about the history of the old airport. He said it was a Second World War airstrip and the battle of the Coral Sea was fought from this strip. Soon we were driving on the old bitumen runway. Trees were starting to grow through the tar and there were still plenty of markers and equipment lying around.

We saw two Palm cockatoos sitting in a tree, so we stopped, and decided to walk for a while. We found three new nests, one had been used this season, and the others had fresh sticks in them. Eddie said the spot he saw birds feeding were just a short distance ahead of us. We came to a clump of Pandanus trees, *Pandanus spiralis*. Fruit was all over the ground, most of the nuts had dried out and only a few were ripe. After close inspection I could see that the birds had been breaking them open to get at the seeds inside. I collected some to take back with me.

Just as we reached the truck we heard what sounded like a chick squawking in a hollow. The size of the hollow was too small for a Palm cockatoo, but it could be all right for an Eclectus parrot, although I was of the opinion this nest was too low. The tree was only about ten feet (3m) high, so Gunter climbed up onto my shoulders and he started to reach in, when a large White-tailed Rat *Uromys caudimaculatus* ran up his arm and up the tree. I don't know who got the biggest shock Gunter or the rat. White-tailed rats are the largest of our native rodents with a body length of just over 13 inches (341mm) plus a 13 inch mosaic tail. The overall length of this large rat was a staggering 27 inches (677mm).

On our way back to our camp Eddie the truck driver said we should call into King Park and see Graham and Ted, which we did. Graham offered us a nice cold beer, which is something you miss while camping out in the tropics. While we were sitting there having a quiet beer or two, I told Graham that we had not seen many birds at nest hollows, and that I thought that the Eclectus parrots had finished before the wet started, possibly back in December, but I thought we would see at least one or two Palm cockatoos nesting through the wet! Ted said, and Graham agreed, that every afternoon a pair of Palm cockatoos landed in a dead tree at the edge of the rainforest about 6pm. We decided to stay and see if they arrived. Sure enough right on six o'clock the Palms arrived. We lay in the shade of the rainforest and watched them for a while, and after about 30 minutes they flew off into the forest. We searched the area but no nest tree was found.

Sunday 9th February was our last day of this five-day scouting trip; we would fly back to Cairns late this afternoon. I checked and repacked the climbing gear as I was storing it at King Park until Oskar and I returned during the next breeding season. Gunter went to finish his sketch of the mine shaft and crusher plant at the old Gordon gold mine.

Although I thought the trip was somewhat disappointing, at least now I knew that the peak-breeding season for the species I wanted to collect was during the months of September, October and November. And as I wanted to collect only fledglings then I would most likely plan to be here sometime towards the middle or end of October.

On the 25th October 1975 Oskar and I were again heading up the Cape. This time we had the company of Helen Brown. Helen Brown was a Naturalist and a local well-known Cairns identity. Although a senior woman, Helen was very active and spent many hours sitting in a hide in her garden studying the Orange-footed Scrubfowl *Megapodius reinwardt*. We became good friends during her twice a week visit to our bird park; she would often bring an armful of native nuts and fruits for our birds.

Helen always wanted to go to Iron Range to study the Scrubfowls there, but never got that chance, until now. Our first night's camp was at the Stewart River after stops at the Split Rock cave paintings and the town of Laura. After dinner that night we heard a Frogmouth calling a short distance up the river. Helen and I thought it sounded different to the Tawny Frogmouth *Podargus strigoides,* so we took the spotlight and decided to see if we could find it. Frogmouths are easy to locate, you just follow their call, then get them in your spotlight. This bird was darker than the Tawny and had bright orange or reddish eyes. We had just sighted our first Marbled Frogmouth *Podargus ocellatus.* This rare sub species was quite a find; it certainly made Helen's night.

The next day was hot and dusty. We were making good time when out of the corner of my eye I saw a large Antilopine Wallaroo *Macropus antilopinus* off to my right about fifty feet into the bush. I glanced down at the speedometer and saw that we were doing 80km (50 mph). This member of the kangaroo family was keeping pace with us and getting closer and closer. I tried going faster but before we knew it "bang" it hit the front right hand mudguard on the Land Rover. The force of the impact sent us off into the bush in a cloud of bulldust; we were lucky not to roll over. The vehicle stopped, the three of us climbed out, there was no sign of the wallaroo.

The damage to the front right hand side of the Land Rover was extensive due to its aluminum construction, but with a little bit of bush repairs with a hammer and axe, we were again on our way. All of us were a little shaken and were now very alert for any wayward wallaroos.

It was 6pm when we reached Yam creek. We could have made it to the Claudie in another three hours, but I didn't want to set up camp in the dark. We sighted our first Palm cockatoo just before we reached Yam creek. I had not camped here before. It was a place we could spend a week if we had the time.

Early next morning before moving on we walked across the creek and looked for Palm cockatoos. We saw quite a few that morning. We also disturbed a small group of them feeding on ripe Pandanus *Pandanus spiralis* fruit that had fallen on the ground. A little further on we watched two Palm cockatoos feeding in a Nonda Plum *Parinari nonda* tree. We gathered some of the fallen fruit. It was ripe, so hopefully our timing for this trip was spot on!

When we reached the Claudie camp site we stopped a short distance before the "spike tree" so we could quietly walk up and check to see if any Eclectus parrots were nesting. As soon as we got close the Shining starlings *Aplonis metallica* flew off in a flock of 100 or more. That number of birds sounded like a gust of wind coming through the rainforest. One female Eclectus parrot *Eclectus roratus macgillivrayi* had her head out of one of the nests. I clapped my hands and out flew two females, and we noticed which nest hollows they flew from.

We set up camp at our old site, excited that this could be the chance that I had thought about all these years. Everything pointed to a good breeding season, so all being well, we would soon have our first baby Eclectus.

The forest was alive with birdcalls; it was great to be back among these unique sounding birds.

After lunch and once the camp was set up we decided to check the area back along the way we had just come. We would walk for an hour then return to camp for a cup of tea, then walk the other way for an hour. This way we would know what birds were nesting in our immediate area. Helen thought this was a good idea because it gave her a chance to become accustomed to the wildlife she was not used to seeing.

Helen could not believe the number of Magnificent Riflebirds *Ptiloris magnificus* that were here in the rainforest. Although we did not sight many we certainly knew they were there. Other species we saw were Spotted Catbird *Ailuroedus melanotis,* Trumpet Manucode *Manucodia keraudrenii,* Black Butcherbird *Cracticus quoyi* and a bird that has a very melodious call, the Olive-backed Oriole *Oriolus sagittatus.*

The first walk back along the track we drove in on did not reveal any new nests. After a cup of tea we were walking for about half an hour along the track to the east of our camp when we heard a female Eclectus parrot making the fluted call about 100 yards (90m) off to our left. I checked my diary notes and map; this must be a new nest, as I did not have any record of it. We walked over towards the spot where we thought the call was coming from. Armed with our binoculars we waited for her to call again, as soon as she did Oskar spotted the tree she was nesting in. It was a very tall Paperbark Tree *Melaleuca leucadendron* on the edge of the rainforest. We made some noise and the female flew out of a hollow on the other side away from us. She landed in a tree a short distance away. Soon her squawking attracted her mate, and he circled us a few times then landed next to the female.

We did not like climbing paperbark trees because the line often became embedded in the soft bark and this made it hard to get the line over. But Oskar and I were keen to give it a go because it felt good to both of us. Paperbark trees can also be dangerous to climb. Although they are a hardwood species they are prone to rot— this is sometimes hard to see under the many layers of paperbark. We decided not to climb this tree until first thing in the morning. I wanted to make sure that if we were lucky enough to collect our first young, I had to be sure that I was prepared and had all I needed to take care of them.

I had brought my handfeeding mixture with me and I also had a box to keep them in, so I was prepared, but I just wanted to double check just to be sure. Early the next morning we drove the vehicle as close to the tree as we could, unloaded the climbing gear onto my shoulders and off we went. The female Eclectus heard us coming: she left the nest and soon both she and the male were flying around us. We tried to be as quick as we could, but we had to be sure that the climb is a safe one. It took me three goes to get the lead over, then after Oskar checked the knots, we both pulled the ladder up, and soon he was on his way up.

Helen had her notebook ready to record the details of what Oskar found; I counted the rungs of the ladder to work out the height of the nest, which was about 65ft (19.8m) high. The nest entrance was facing to the northeast. The tree was a *Melaleuca leucadendron* paperbark tree on the edge of the rainforest.

We waited until Oskar had inspected the nest cavity. He reached into his bag and got his flashlight, a few moments later he called out "two chicks". I called out to him what age were they? He said not very old, maybe five days or so. Now I had to decide to take them or leave them. If I decided to leave them until the last day before we returned to Cairns then I risked the female deserting them or losing them to a predator. If I take them now, can I keep them warm enough at night?

Oskar started to climb down so we could decide what we should do, but before he had reached the ground I said we would take them now. Oskar said he would need a scoop because the nest was about 4ft (1.2m) deep. I had a scoop in my equipment bag. He climbed back up and after a few minutes descended with our first *Eclectus roratus macgillivrayi*.

Returning to the ground Oskar handed me the bag containing the two Eclectus chicks. I opened the bag to see two healthy chicks about seven days old; they were naked and both had full crops. I gave them to Helen to hold while Oskar and I lowered the ladder and gathered up our gear. On returning to the vehicle Oskar gave me the rest of the details about the nest. Nest entrance size 5 inches (127mm), nesting material, could not feel due to the depth of nest, but it appeared moist and he could see quite a few feathers in the nest with the flashlight. Oskar thought this was a well-used nest.

Just before we returned to camp we noticed the female return and enter her nest, I said we should check this nest again before we leave to see if she lays a second clutch.

Back at camp I placed the two chicks in the box that I had already placed nesting material in. I also left one of the woolen bags around them for warmth. These bags were made out of a woolen blanket material and were great for keeping babies of this age warm. Because their crops were full, I noted the time; I would wait until they were empty, which could take three or four hours. Now I had to decide where I was going to leave them while we were out collecting.

While we were in camp I would leave them on the front seat of the Land Rover, this would be the safest place especially at night, and there they would be safe from white-tailed rats, pythons and owls. During the day while we were away collecting was the problem; we could not take them with us so I had to come up with a safe place. Because of the heat we did not use tents to sleep in, we just had a large tarpaulin tied to trees to stop the dew during the night, and it gave us plenty of shade during the day.

I always carried a few meters of birdwire with me on these trips and I had some small weldmesh panels that I pre cut back in Cairns. I decided to make up one of these cages that would be large enough to take the box containing the babies. This worked out extremely well. The top of this cage was the door and I just had to fold it back and place the bird box in. Then when we were away I would close the cage up and place something heavy on top and they were safe.

We decided to climb the "spike tree" as it was only walking distance away and I could check on how the chicks were doing in their new surroundings. The spike tree is one of the highest and hardest trees to climb. It took me at least five shots to get the lead over the branch, where Oskar wanted the ladder to go, but once the lead went over it only took a few minutes to pull the ladder up. The Shining starlings took off in a cloud of blue/black feathers flying 100 meters above us; they looked like a swarm of black insects at that distance. We had not noticed before that the White Goshawk *Accipiter novaehollandiae* was also nesting in the leafy branches of this fig tree.

Before long Oskar was checking the first nest hollow, "two fresh eggs" he called out. He then proceeded to the second nest higher up the ladder, again "two eggs". These were about half developed, he said. Oskar returned to the ground. After he caught his breath he gave me the details for my diary, the third nest he thought still contained water. He could see small birds entering and coming out wet, so they were bathing in this hollow, also birds would most likely enter this hollow to drink. I was not interested in removing eggs for incubation because of the distance they would have to travel and it was not a condition of my collecting permit. I felt that we would be successful in collecting the required number of chicks.

We lowered the ladder and walked back to camp. The two chicks were okay, their crops still contained food so I would leave them and check them again in a couple of hours. After lunch I decided to stay back at camp to feed the two Eclectus chicks and to catch up on my notes. Oskar and Helen decided to drive down to the old Gordon mine area and have a look around there.

Later in the afternoon I made up the handfeeding mixture and fed the two Eclectus chicks. They were slow at first but soon were feeding well, and their droppings looked okay. I changed the paper towel they were sitting on so I could monitor their next lot of droppings to see if their new diet went through properly. They seemed to have adapted quickly to the warmth of the cardboard box.

Oskar and Helen returned from their scouting trip with news of another Eclectus parrots'nest near the old gold mine. I showed them my map of recorded nests and this one appeared to be another new one. It was getting late in the day so we decided to climb it tomorrow morning. While we were having dinner that evening we discussed moving our camp down to the Top Pascoe track, as this would save us a lot of traveling back and forth to feed the babies.

Late that night just after I had fed the babies and I had just got into bed I heard sounds coming from behind our camp. It was just after midnight, about fifteen minutes later I heard the noise again. This time I was sure it was wild pigs scrounging for food among the leaf matter on the rainforest floor. I reached for my rifle, just in case. I gave Oskar a nudge, but he had heard the noise as well and was awake. Then the mob of pigs must have got our scent. All hell broke loose, and instead of the pigs turning and running in the other direction they decided to charge straight through our camp. I got off a couple of shots hoping to disperse them, but they came right through the middle of us. Poor Helen did not know what was going on. After the mob of pigs (about fifteen of them) left we tried to survey the damage they caused. Thankfully the two chicks were in the cabin of the Land Rover. Apart from fallen tarps and camping gear all over the place we were all okay. Helen thought it was a great thrill.

The next morning we packed up and climbed the new nest on our way to our new campsite. We drove off the main track to Portland Roads and headed up along an old mining track to where Helen and Oskar found the nest the day before. I parked the vehicle a few hundred meters before the nest so we could walk up slowly to see if the female was sitting. A large male Eclectus parrot saw us and began squawking as he flew over us. Oskar pointed to the nest high in a fig tree right on the edge of the rainforest. This tree was also growing on the edge of a steep gully, it would be difficult to get a clear shot, but it was worth a try.

By this time the female had left the nest and was flying around us accompanied by this beautiful large male, I drove the vehicle up as close as I could and got out the climbing gear, I estimated the height of this nest to be over 100ft (30m) from the ground. I laid out a hessian bag on the ground so I could coil out some loose fishing line on it; this would give me more distance with the shot, as the lead would travel quicker.

Everything was ready, my first shot was a good one, right between the fork just above the nest hollow, twenty minutes later the ladder was in position and Oskar was on his way up. The nest was difficult to reach and Oskar had to leave the ladder. I was never comfortable with a climber leaving the ladder because while I was holding the ladder I could feel every movement he made and I had some idea of how the climber felt even if I could not see him. I called out to Oskar, "Are you sure you have to get off the ladder?" "Yes" came his reply. I waited until I felt he had left the ladder and was now on his own high in the crown of this fig tree. I called out, "We're letting the ladder go so we can walk out to see you." "Okay" Oskar called out. Helen and I walked out onto the track to watch Oskar at work. He was sitting in the fork of the tree deciding how to reach down and inspect this nest. He decided that if I untied the ladder and took its weight he could lift it out further along the branch. I could then retie it; he then could climb back onto the ladder and would be in a better position to reach the nest. My only problem with this idea was the ladder would sag quite a lot once he returned to it, and there was a chance the ladder would twist. I explained this to Oskar and he said it would be all right. I untied the rope holding the ladder and he managed to move it into its new position further out along the branch. Helen and I tied it off and I climbed up a few meters to take the slack out of it.

I called out to Oskar that I thought it was now safe to climb back on, I was back holding the ladder and could tell when he was back on and safe. He inspected the nest to find two freshly laid eggs, he returned to the ground; we lowered the ladder and returned to the vehicle as quickly as we could. I backed the vehicle up a few hundred meters and we watched to see if the female returned to her nest. After all was quiet she returned.

Oskar gave me the details of this nest for my diary; I also marked the nest on my map. The height of this nest was just over 90ft (27.5m). The size of the nest entrance was eight inches (203mm), and it was only eighteen inches deep (457mm); the nesting material was dry/moist wood dust; there was a number of female feathers lining the nest; it contained two fresh laid eggs.

We arrived at our new campsite mid morning. We found an area in the open forest that had been recently burnt out (Aboriginals and Stockmen burn the grass during the dry season to stimulate growth). It would be a safe place to camp; there was a small creek close by. After we had set up camp we had an early lunch. I fed the babies and set them up under the tarp in the shade. It was a lot hotter here in the open; the rainforest camp was at least ten degrees cooler. With the weather so hot we decided to have a siesta during the hottest part of the day.

Later in the afternoon we walked along the track for an hour or so; every now and then we would dart off into the bush to inspect a possible nesting tree. If there were no birds present we would tap the base of the tree to see if a sitting female would flush. To our surprise one of these trees had a Palm cockatoo *Probosciger aterrimus macgillivrayi* nesting in it, and when we tapped the base out she flew. Competition for nesting hollows between the Sulphur-crested Cockatoo *Cacatua galerita* and Palm cockatoos must be great, with the Sulphur-crested cockatoo winning against the more timid Palm. I saw this many times. Palms would work a nest for weeks, to then have it taken over by the more aggressive Sulphur-crested. This nest was so low we couldn't believe it. This nest was only 10ft (3m) high. Oskar only had to stand on my shoulders to be able to look in. To our further surprise there was a half grown almost fully feathered Palm cockatoo chick inside. I decided to leave it for a few days and collect it the day we left to return to Cairns.

We spent the next few days inspecting the known nests in that area of the Top Pascoe track without success. Any nest that was active only had eggs. I had to decide whether to stay a longer period to have any hope of obtaining more chicks, or return to Cairns with the two Eclectus and the one Palm cockatoo and then try and come again at the end of November. If a trip was planned at the end of next month, I ran the risk of storms and the start of the wet season.

I decided that "a bird in the hand was worth two in the bush," a quote Helen made to me was the best option. We would pack up and return to Cairns the next day. Next morning we were all up early, had breakfast and packed up our gear, loaded the vehicle and drove to the

Palm cockatoo's nest. I managed to get the front of the vehicle up against the tree, Oskar reached in and removed the baby Palm. We placed it into another cardboard box with nesting material and Helen supported it on her lap for the long drive south. The two baby Eclectus chicks were in their box on the floor behind Oskar's legs sitting on a pillow to stop any jarring.

The drive out was slow as we did not want to upset the babies too much. The young Palm was remarkably quiet and tame. Its crop was about half full so we would feed it when we stopped for lunch.

Our return trip south to Cairns took three days, with overnight stops at the Hann and Laura rivers. All three babies fed extremely well and the rough dusty drive did not seem to upset them in any way. Late on the third afternoon we arrived at our bird park— although it's good to get away into the Australian bush it's even better to be home. Helen told my wife that it was the greatest and most enjoyable experience of her life.

Post script to the 1975 trip: All three birds were successfully raised, the two Eclectus parrots fledged into a male and female and were beautiful large birds. The Palm cockatoo, who I named "Pascoe," was a joy to raise. He (I thought he was a male) was so tame and would later become a favorite with the hundreds of local school children who attended the park on school excursions. He was housed in a large flight aviary and when I took these school children on a tour of our park and I entered his aviary, he would fly down and land on my shoulder.

Due to a busy tourist season and work commitments I was unable to return to Cape York that year, but it was always on my mind. Every spare minute was spent planning and checking my notes, and soon I was keen to head north again.

Because I was unable to go up the Cape in the latter part of 1975, and as every wet season is different, I would now have to do a scouting trip early in the dry season to get a feel for the coming breeding season. I decided to go at the end of August of 1976. Oskar was unavailable due to his work so I took a mate of mine from Palm Cove, Gary Grant. Gary and I met while spearfishing on a diving trip to the outer Barrier Reef.

On the 29th of August 1976 Gary and I departed Cairns for Iron Range. The reason for this trip was twofold: (1) we had to check the breeding season to work out what would be the best time to collect chicks from the nest. Would this breeding season be early or later than last year? Each year is different depending on the wet season; if the wet season is a short somewhat dry season then the breeding season will be early; if it's too dry and there is not a lot of food available they may not nest at all. (2) ABC television (Australian Broadcasting Corporation) wanted to do a documentary about me and collecting for their series of "Big Country"; this series was about Australians with unusual occupations. I thought this would be great publicity for our bird park.

The three days we spent checking our trees around the Claudie River and both the top and bottom Pascoe tracks convinced me that the month of November would be the best time to come. To me it appeared to be a later nesting season than last year. We never saw any Eclectus at their nests and Palm cockatoos were still working their hollows. It was wetter than last year as the rivers were higher. I had never been to Cape York in November before. We could be risking getting caught in early storms, and there was a chance that if the wet season started early we might not be able to drive back out.

I was prepared to take that risk, and if we got cut off by the heavy rain then I would leave my vehicle at King Park and fly out.

Before Gary and I left Iron Range we saw Ron who said he would keep his eye out for nesting Palms and Eclectus parrots. That would be a great help to me to have someone spotting for me. On arrival back at Cairns I started plans for the November expedition.

On the 5th of November 1976 Gary and I, the ABC producer and reporter left Cairns in two Land Rovers for Iron Range. Three days later three others, the cameraman, his assistant and soundman, would arrive by air at Iron Range airport.

I had arranged with Peter Hybis, the owner of King Park, for us to camp at the cattle station. We set up large tarpaulins on the lawn behind the main homestead; there the TV crew would at least have electric power and hot showers.

Soon after arriving at King Park we drove down to Portlands Roads to show the television producer some of the local scenery and to catch up with Ron. Ron was again out fishing but was due back shortly, so we decided to wait. While we were waiting we walked up to some of the old World War Two gun emplacements. These large concrete bunkers were built to stop the pending Japanese invasion during that war. They were high up, cut into the side of the hill overlooking the beach. We could see for miles, and we could also see Ron in his boat heading back to the jetty.

Ron had been fishing since early morning and had a nice catch of coral trout. These are one of the nicest fish on the reef to eat; he gave us a few to take back to King Park. After I introduced the others to him over a cup of tea, Ron said do you want another baby Palm cockatoo! I looked at the TV producer who got very excited." That's great," he said, "As soon as the rest of the crew arrives we will film it." I asked Ron was this the nest along the bottom Pascoe track we looked at last August. "That's it," he said. I was happy and slightly relieved I had promised David the producer at least one Palm cockatoo to film.

On the way back to King Park I pointed out to David the track that led to Ron's Palm cockatoo nest. I also stopped near the "69tree". We walked in to have a look, and a Sulphur-crested Cockatoo *Cacatua galerita* flew out. I said he could film us climbing this one if he liked, as it will have some young "white cockies" in it. David said he would make a note of it.

The next morning was spent showing the producer and the reporter other areas that I thought would be of interest to them. The plane was due in at 11am with the rest of the TV crew so I took them down past the airport to the causeway to show them where I thought they could get good shots of us climbing. On our way back we saw the plane approaching the runway. We reached the airport just as they were leaving the plane. After the introductions we loaded their camera gear and headed for King Park.

We started filming after lunch— shots of Gary and me driving around, unloading the climbing gear, then putting it back on the back of the Land Rover and driving around some more. This took most of the afternoon. The next day we would start climbing, so Gary and I worked till late in the evening checking all our climbing gear.

After a quick breakfast we headed down to Portland Roads to pick up Ron and climb the Palm cockatoo's nest he found along the bottom Pascoe track. Ron was expecting us and was waiting at the front of his house; I introduced the rest of the TV crew to him and then drove him to the tree. David the producer wanted to try and get some shots of the bird leaving the nest so we parked the two vehicles in the bush a few hundred meters before the tree. I led them to a position where they could get a good clear shot of the female leaving the nest, I said give me a nod when you want Gary and me to walk up and tap the tree.

After a couple of minutes they were set up and gave the nod to walk in. Gary led the way; I followed carrying the ladder on my shoulder. When we reached the tree Gary tapped it with a stick. We could hear the female starting to make her way up the inside of the nest. At first she just stuck her head out to see what the noise was, then she saw us and climbed out, sat for a couple of seconds then flew off in the direction of the camera.

Gary and I started to get the climbing gear ready. David came over and said that they got some excellent shots of the cockatoo. They set up to film us climbing this tree. This tree was not very high, about 20 feet (6m) and not very stable, it was just a dead stump really, but because of the competition between the Palms and the Sulphur-crested cockatoos they have take what they can get. We had to tie off this tree so it could support Gary's weight and the weight of the ladder. It only took Gary a few minutes to climb this nest; he soon was back on the ground with a healthy baby Palm Cockatoo *Probosciger aterrimus macgillivrayi*.

The young Palm was about six weeks old and feathered, its crest just starting to grow. They are such gentle birds. Gary said the nest was only about 3ft (900mm) deep and he could just reach it, the nesting material was splintered twigs and quite dry.

We drove Ron back to the port, had a cup of tea with him and did some filming of the beach and jetty. On our way back to King Park we climbed another three nests of Palm cockatoos without success. All three were good nests and were being used, but either they have not laid yet or the young had already left the nest I reminded David about the 69 tree, and did he want to film us climbing it. He said we might just as well seeing we are here. We stopped a short distance from the nest, walked in quietly, the TV crew set up and we made some noise. The female white cockatoo flew out, and Gary and I set up to climb it. The nest contained two almost fully grown chicks. Gary removed both chicks so they could film them, a couple of the crew wanted to try their hand at climbing the tree— one was successful, the other only got half way up the ladder. It always looks easier when someone else does it. Gary returned the two chicks to the nest hollow; we packed up and returned to King Park.

We found a large cardboard box at the homestead to put the young Palm in. A short time later Peter Hybis arrived back with two of his men and told us they thought they also had a Palm's nest. One of the station hands whose nickname was "Bromly" (why he was called Bromly I cannot recall) said he saw this black bird fly out while he was mustering cattle a few days ago. We said that we would go out and climb it after lunch.

We followed the station's Toyota land-cruiser along this track to the east of the homestead; this was a new track to me, so I made sure I noted it in my diary for the future. We must have traveled about 5km. When the Toyota ahead of us stopped, we all got out and walked a short distance to this tall Bloodwood tree *Eucalyptus polycarpa* that was standing in open forest about 100 feet (30m) from the edge of the Rainforest. There were no birds present and when I tapped the tree nothing flew out. I still wanted to climb it so we went back to the vehicles and drove them closer. They also decided to film Gary making the climb.

I estimated the height of this nest at around 23feet (7m) high. I managed to get the lead sinker over with my first shot, soon the ladder was up and Garry was ready to climb. I thought this nest would have been good for white cockatoos and I was surprised when Garry called out that it contained an almost fully-grown Palm cockatoo.

Garry had a bit of trouble in getting the quite large chick into his bag, but he lowered it down with its head sticking out. It was a lot bigger chick than the one we got earlier, still these birds are remarkably tame and made no attempt to bite.

On our return to King Park I placed the two Palms together. They accepted each other straight away. I had only one Palm cockatoo left to collect on my permit quota, plus two Eclectus parrots and four Red-cheeked parrots *Geoffroyus geoffroyi* plus four Marshall's Fig parrots *Cyclopsitta diophthalma marshalli*. First thing tomorrow we would concentrate on Eclectus parrots, then if time permitted do some work on the Red-cheeks. Later that afternoon the young Palm cockatoos fed well. You would think I'd had them for a couple of weeks rather than just one day.

Next morning after I'd fed the birds again we decided to climb the "spike tree." This would be a real test for Gary. David wanted a high tree in the rainforest for the next segment of his film, plus he was hoping to get some good shots of Eclectus parrots flying around and landing in the tree. Gary, I knew, was nervous about such a high climb but assured me he was up to it.

Everybody from King Park wanted to come and see us climb this tree. David the producer said it would be okay as long as they all stayed out of the way and kept quiet while they were filming. When we arrived at the bank of the middle Claudie River we parked the three vehicles off the road, unloaded our climbing and camera gear and slowly walked across the river. As we approached the tree I asked David if he wanted to set up first to try and get a shot of the female leaving the nest. He said that was a good idea, so I beckoned to the others to wait and be quiet while I got the camera crew into position. We diverted through the rainforest so the nesting birds would not see or hear us. Once the Shining Starlings *Aplonis metallica* heard us then the alarm would be raised and we could lose the chance to film the Eclectus parrots leaving their nests.

I managed to get the camera crew set up and as soon as they were ready Gary and I carried the climbing gear to the base of the "spike tree." The White Goshawk *Accipiter novaehollandiae* gave the alarm first. Then as predicted the whole flock of Shining starlings flew off in a mad panic, followed by the nesting female Eclectus parrots who paused briefly at the entrance to their nest hollows, before joining the rest of the noise makers in circling us at a great height. David joined Gary and me at the base of the tree. He said they got some good shots of the females at their nest. He said that the cameramen would stay where they were and film Gary and me rigging up the ladder and Gary climbing.

By this time the others from King Park had joined us and were watching us from the track. I came out to where they were to make the shot with the "Shanghai"; I laid out the hessian bag so I could spool off some fishing line and was ready to make my first shot. One of the film crew was laying down on the edge of the scrub. I said, be careful lying there you might catch "scrub mite." I think he thought I was joking. I made my first of five misses. This tree is high. Gary was probably hoping I would just keep on missing. My sixth shot found its mark and after a bit of trouble in finding the lead sinker, the ladder was on its way up. The position of the ladder was exactly the position we had it last time, so I knew it would at least give Gary a chance to inspect two nests.

Once the ladder was up and safely tied off, both Gary and I jumped on together to test that it would not slip back. We walked out to the others waiting on the track. The film crew guy was still lying on the ground. I said, do you think I was joking about the scrub mite? He said yes. Well I wasn't, scrub mite is a microscopic mite that infests the nest of those Shining starlings up there. I pointed to the mass of nests these birds make in the uppermost branches of this giant fig tree. Then I pointed to the many fallen nests strewn all over the ground; he was lying within arm's reach of these nests. I said if you want to lay down then lay down on the road, he took no notice of me. Later that night he would wish he had taken my advice.

Gary was ready to climb, I told him this is going to be the hardest climb you will ever make, please just take your time, don't worry about the camera, and just concentrate on the climb and rest when you need to. The first part of the climb would be the toughest; it was 60ft (18m) to the first branch and 115ft (34m) to the first nest. Everyone was ready; I anchored the ropes tied to the bottom of the ladder and boosted Gary up to the first rung. He was on his way, he reached about halfway then stopped to have a rest (climbing straight up vertically puts a lot of pressure on your arms and shoulders). I called out to him "which aches the most, your arms or legs?" He said his arms hurt. I called out, have a rest then climb using your legs. After a few minutes he started to make his way up the ladder. Soon he had made it to the fork in the tree that the ladder went through. He then left the ladder and sat in the fork of the tree. It is extremely hard for Gary to hear us with all the noise coming from the Shining starlings and the eight Eclectus parrots flying around him.

I gestured to Gary to have a rest before he decided to try and reach the first nest, which was higher up the tree. Five minutes passed and he was ready to climb further up the tree to the Eclectus nest. Leaving the ladder meant he was on his own and he had to be extremely careful—these trees are at the best of times very slippery. He reached the nest without any problems and on inspection called out "two chicks". I signaled to him to remove them and come back down. On his way down the ladder he passed the lowest nest that was in the main trunk. He asked me to pull him in closer to the tree. One of the cattle station hands gave me a hand and we managed to get Garry close enough to have a look in. "Another two chicks," he called out. I said I already have my quota, so come on down.

On returning to the safety of "terra firma" Gary had the shakes. He said that was the highest climb that I have ever made. He hoped there were no more trees like that. I said well done, you are one of the very few that have climbed the "spike tree." Once Garry had caught his breath, I asked him which chicks were older, the ones he removed or the ones we left in the nest. He said the ones back in the nest looked older to him, then he said you don't want me to swap them over do you? I thought about it for a while, then I said that I only wanted to see the look on your face.

The two chicks Gary removed had not long broken color and were about five weeks old, another male and female. This could not have worked out better for me as I had two (hopefully) unrelated pairs of Australian Eclectus parrots.

We packed up the gear and returned to our camp at King Park. I fed the young Palm cockatoos and checked the crops of the Eclectus parrots, which were full; all the babies were doing well. Over lunch I told David the producer to keep an eye on one of his men who was laying down under the tree, just let me know if he starts feeling itchy or you see him scratching.

Scrub mite is one of the few things I fear in the rainforest. Once it infests your clothes or gets on your skin it's hard to eradicate. I am sure it is transmitted in the droppings of the Shining Starlings *Aplonis metallica* and infests their nests. On one of my previous trips up here, a birdwatcher was observing these Starlings from under the tree as we drove past. We stopped to see what he was looking at, and I noticed that he had a few starling droppings on his shirt. Later the next day we heard he had to be flown back to Cairns for emergency treatment— his whole body had become swollen and was covered in a nasty rash, his eyes were just slits; he was in hospital for ten days. Scrub mite cannot be seen by the naked eye, it's microscopic and gets into the pores of your skin where it's starts eating away at you. You start to itch and scratch which only inflames the problem. One of the old time prospectors I met on that same trip told me, the only way to prevent the mites biting you was to wash every night with "Dettol ™ Antiseptic Solution" which contains 4.8 percent Chloroxlenol. And to also wash all our clothes in a plastic bucket containing a cap full of the Dettol in the water. That was back in 1969 and I have been using it on every trip since. I always carry a bottle in my camping gear.

Later in the afternoon David the producer and I decided to drive out along the old Lockhart Mission road to do some final filming. The camera crew was due to fly out the next afternoon and he wanted to get some shots of us climbing trees in the open forest. I said that as I had my quota of Eclectus parrots I would now turn my attention to the Red-cheeked Parrot *Geoffroyus geoffroyi* and the last Palm cockatoo. We climbed about three or four cockatoo nests without any luck and we were about to turn back when I heard Red-cheeks calling on the other side of a strip of rainforest. I stopped the vehicles on the edge of the rainforest out of sight of the birds and gestured to the others to be quiet and to get out and walk behind me. With binoculars in hand I went looking for these rare parrots. They saw me before I spotted them, sitting high in a dead tree, the female at a nest hollow that she had excavated. Through the binoculars I could see that they were a beautiful pair of birds.

The TV crew set up to get them on film. These parrots took no notice of us and never attempted to fly away. The tree they were nesting in was too rotten and unsafe to climb and although I would have loved to be able to inspect their nest it was not to be.

On arrival back at King Park I fed all the babies. One of the Palm cockatoos was sitting on the edge of their box waiting to be fed. I was looking forward to getting them home, where I could better care for them. The long dry dusty drive was ahead of us. While we were having dinner that night I noticed the camera crew guy starting to scratch himself. I said to him, "Take off your shirt." Why, he asked, "So I can have a look at your skin." He took off his shirt. He was covered in a red rash starting on his back and spreading to his chest. I said you should have told me earlier, those scrub mites have bitten you.

I told him to take off all his clothes he wore that day and place them in a bucket of hot water. I added some Dettol to the water. I then told him to go and have a hot shower at the homestead. I also told him when he was finished to fill a bucket up with warm water and add a full cap full of Dettol, then pour it over him, don't rinse it off, and just allow it to dry. By next morning the rash was gone and he was very thankful for the help.

Today was our last day; the film crew that flew in just a few days ago would fly out after lunch, which left David and the reporter, Gary and I to drive out. We did some final filming that morning, mainly driving past the camera and some background shots, and a segment of me feeding the four babies completed the job.

We broke camp just before lunch. The first thunder storms were building up behind Mount Tozer. It was time to leave this fascinating and incredible place. We loaded the camping gear onto the two Land Rovers, said our good-byes to Peter Hybis and his men at King Park, then drove the rest of the film crew to the airport to catch their flight back south to Cairns.

In two hours they would be sitting back in their air conditioned hotels while we faced a further three days driving out. For me, I loved the bush and always looked forward to the drive. Although hot, dry and very dusty, it was exciting and with the storms building could also be challenging.

We made it through to the Archer River that night. We had two heavy downpours of rain, a lot of thunder and lightning, but the track held up and the rivers had not started to rise as yet. When we arrived at the Archer it was again fine and dry; the storms must have been isolated around Mount Tozer and Iron Range. We had a nice swim in the cool waters of the Archer; the four babies traveled and were feeding well.

The next day was extremely hot, there was no breeze at all, and every creek we came to we just fell in to cool off. The heat was affecting the baby birds as well. When we stopped for lunch we decided to spend the hottest part of the day under trees in the river and wait until it started to cool down in the afternoon. About 3pm there were storms forming to the east of us and a nice breeze had arrived. It was time to push on. I fed the babies then we drove to the Palmer River and camped for the night.

There was no rain during the night, but there were plenty of storms to the north and east. On reaching the Palmer River we were now out of danger of being cut off by early storms. We had gambled on getting through and it had paid off. The road home, although still gravel, was a graded one and an all weather road.

Midday the next day we were home. Over a cup of tea at the bird park we said goodbye to David and his reporter and he said he would contact me when the series would go to air, and they left. I fed the babies who were already popular with some of our park visitors, who saw them sitting in their cardboard boxes on the floor of my office.

Between 1977 and 1985 I would do further bird watching trips to Cape York to study these magnificent parrots. The four birds I collected fledged into beautiful large birds, and I was told later that they were among the first (official) *Eclectus roratus macgillivrayi* in captivity. It would be another ten years before I would successfully breed these beautiful parrots.

Bird watching and collecting in the wild has taught me so much about how we as breeders of these birds should care for them in captivity. These unique parrots from the tropical rainforests of Australia, New Guinea, the Solomon Islands and Indonesia do require special care and housing. They are birds of the rainforest canopy; their diet consists of tropical fruits, nuts and blossoms and seeds that they can forage from these rainforests. If we feed them as close to their natural diet as we can in captivity, by providing a daily balanced fruit and vegetable diet they are long lived and extremely good breeders.

Chapter 4
The Captive Breeding of Eclectus Parrots

On16th June 1988 in Monaco, at a Sotheby's auction, a collection of fine paintings by the French artist *Jacques Barraband* (1767-1768 to 1809) were offered for sale. Held at the famous casino of Monte Carlo this collection of 94 watercolour paintings was part of over 300 finished watercolours of birds. Among this unique collection of his work for *Francois Le Vaillants* Histoire Naturelle des Perroquets and Histoire Naturelle des Oiseaux de Paradis were two paintings of Eclectus parrots.

Lot 176 described as *Perroquet Grand Lori* was a watercolour painting 520mm by 400mm (20 by 16 inches) of a female Vosmaeri Eclectus Parrot, *Eclectus roratus vosmaeri*. Lot 193 described as *Perroquet a Flancs Rouges* was of a male Red-Sided Eclectus Parrot, *Eclectus roratus polychloros*. This watercolor painting was the same size as the first painting.

These two exquisite French paintings, most likely painted using museum skins show that Eclectus parrots could have arrived in Europe around 1760, over two hundred and forty years ago. Most bird books of the modern era state that the first breeding of Eclectus Parrots occurred in Germany in 1881, followed by England in 1912 and San Diego Zoo in 1929.

There was no recorded breeding of Eclectus parrots for over a hundred years. This would be because they were thought to be two separate species, so they housed two green birds together thinking they were male and female, the same was for the two red birds. Even today when friends of mine see my Eclectus parrots for the first time, they have trouble in believing that they are of the same species. So it's not to hard to understand the predicament a bird curator may have had at one of these early European Zoos when a shipment of new birds arrived from the Far East with one box containing green birds and the other containing red ones.

For more than two hundred and forty years Eclectus parrots have been kept either as pets or in captive breeding situations throughout the world. When these beautiful and unusual parrots were first collected from the Moluccas by early spice traders then taken to Europe, they were thought to be members of the lory family. Was it because of their fine tight feathering that they resembled Lories?

It wasn't until the Ornithologist A.B Meyer arrived back in Europe claiming that these red and blue, green and red birds, were the same species. He was not believed at first. Many of the skins in museums had not been sexed correctly; it took a few years before his claims were accepted (Iredale, 1956).

Today the Eclectus parrot is well established in aviculture with hundreds bred each year, most find their way back into aviculture with new breeders wanting to try something new, and others enter the pet trade. Eclectus parrots over the last ten years have become very popular as household pets.

4.1 Purchasing an Eclectus Parrot

Before deciding to purchase an Eclectus parrot, what are some of the pitfalls? What do we look out for? What do we feed them on? These are just a few of the important questions that we should ask ourselves before making our first purchase.

First we should learn all we can about the housing and keeping of Eclectus parrots. Join a local bird club or avicultural society, visit the local library and read up about these fascinating birds. Another good place to start looking for information about these birds is via the internet, just log on and type in Eclectus parrot and you will be amazed at the amount of information that is made available. Many breeders of these birds have their own web sites and can be contacted by email. These sites contain photos as well as a host of useful information on keeping and breeding these birds; one web address that I do recommend is the Eclectus Group at http://www.lgd.org/eclectusgroup. Once we feel that we are confident enough to care for these birds then it's time to start looking around. Visit the local pet shop, ask questions about their care and feeding, find out if there are any Eclectus parrot breeders in the area. If there is, then phone them and make an appointment to visit them. Most reputable breeders welcome newcomers to their aviaries. Visit more than one breeder— this will help to better understand how these birds are kept.

By joining a local bird club or avicultural society we can meet other people that share the same interests in the keeping of Eclectus parrots. The prices of Eclectus parrots vary from country to country and state to state, so it pays to shop around. By being a member of a local bird club it doesn't take long to gain an understanding of prices.

Deciding what sub species to keep is the next question that faces us. If the Eclectus parrot being purchased is just to be kept as a single bird as a pet, then it doesn't really matter which sub species is chosen, although most likely it would be one of the sub species that are specially bred for the pet market, like the Red-sided Eclectus Parrot *Eclectus roratus polychloros*, or crossbred birds. Deciding whether it be a male or female pet Eclectus parrot comes down to personal choice, as both male and female make excellent pets, and both sexes learn to say a few words.

If a pair or pairs of Eclectus parrots are being considered then a lot more thought has to be put into the choice of sub species. A few years ago Eclectus were just "Eclectus", one red one and one green one meant you had a pair of Eclectus parrots, but of an unknown sub species. Nowadays most experienced breeders of Eclectus parrots are "species specific" and breed only pure birds. Price will also determine which sub species is kept. If keeping Eclectus parrots for the first time then it's recommended that starting off with the Red sided or New Guinea Eclectus, *Eclectus roratus polychloros,* as they are the most common kept sub species, and the easiest to obtain.

When purchasing Eclectus parrots I prefer to purchase them from other Eclectus breeders, usually someone who is known to me. I rarely purchase breeding pairs from bird dealers or pet stores because of two reasons: (1) they offer little or no background history of the birds they have for sale; if you ask them if they have bred before they will always answer yes, and if you ask how old they are they, the answer is "young, just starting to breed." (2) If I see a beautiful pair of adult Eclectus parrots for sale at a pet store, the very first question I ask myself is "If these birds are a breeding pair, then why are they here?" Eclectus breeders don't sell breeding pairs to pet stores; they are sold to other Eclectus breeders!

This is not to say that I am anti pet stores or bird dealers, they have an important role to play in the avicultural industry. Many bird breeders of other species of parrots, cockatoos and finches breed exclusively for these outlets and more importantly it's the bird dealers and pet stores that set the retail prices for birds.

Once deciding to purchase a pair or pairs of Eclectus parrots, it's recommended purchasing only purebred birds. This is again why we should purchase our birds from specialist Eclectus parrot breeders. By purchasing from breeders that keep and breed pure birds we should at least be assured of getting a pair of birds of the same sub species.

4.2 Housing

Housing of Eclectus parrots will depend on the number of pairs being kept. If a first time breeder of these birds it's important to build their aviary to suit the environment in which they will live. If living in a cold climate then it's important to understand that these birds are a tropical species and are used to high temperature and humidity. Although they will adapt and breed in cold climates, care should be taken to make sure that they are out of cold drafts and they get as much early morning sun as possible.

Here in Australia most aviaries are constructed facing the northeast, this way they get the early morning sun. Most of our cold prevailing winds come from the south or southwest. The size of the aviary depends on the area that is available. If keeping one pair per aviary then the size of the aviary should be 30ft.long by 6ft.wide by 7ft.high, (9.1m long by 1.8m wide by 2.1m high). These aviaries are usually built in banks of eight or twelve. There is an access passageway to the rear shelter area; this should be a minimum of 4ft (1.2m) wide. I prefer 6ft (1.8m.) wide so I can enter with a wheelbarrow for cleaning and it gives me plenty of room to turn around. The shelter area of the aviary is 6ft (1.8m.) square. Both the floors of the access passageway and shelter area should be concrete for easy cleaning and washing down.

The roof size of the covered access passageway and shelter area is 13ft (3.9m). This allows for a 1ft (305mm) overhang for rainwater run off. This means that the actual open flight area is 18ft (5.4m) long.

The rear wall of the passageway (facing the direction of the cold prevailing winds) is fully enclosed with either panel iron sheets or brick construction. The sides in line with the size of the shelter area is also covered; this gives each pair full protection from the cold, it also gives the breeding pairs privacy.

The size of the wire mesh used for keeping Eclectus parrots is in my view extremely important, too small a mesh could cause damage to beaks, too large a mesh could result in death. (A friend of mine decided to keep a pair of Eclectus parrots in two-inch chain link mesh. these birds would always put their heads through the mesh and take food from his hand. One morning he found the female dead with her head caught through one hole and her beak hooked through another.)

Over the years I have tried all sizes of wire mesh. I have found that one-inch by one-inch (25mm by 25mm) by 1.6mm diameter mesh the best for keeping Eclectus parrots in. This size mesh is easy to work with and is easily clipped together by using "J" clips.

All internal walls between flights are double wired to prevent toe biting and fighting between pairs. All new wire should be treated with a solution of one part vinegar to two parts of water to prevent "new wire disease." If birds are placed into new aviaries that have not been treated then they run the risk of ingesting zinc powder from new wire; this is done by licking the wire with their tongues. This fine white powder tastes like salt to the birds and if not removed could prove deadly. Once the wire is treated leave it for 30 minutes then rinse off with fresh water.

Just as important is choosing the right material and size of perch for the aviary. I prefer to use natural tree branches of various sizes, ranging from ¾ of an inch to two and a half inches in diameter. This gives the birds the chance to perch where it's the most comfortable and the thicker part of the perch can be used for mating. The perches I use are from eucalyptus trees and are replaced every few months. Eclectus parrots are not destructive in any way and when new eucalyptus perches are replaced they enjoy stripping off and eating the bark. Once or twice a week I would also place a bunch of fresh cut eucalyptus bush containing buds and blossoms for them to eat and play in.

The foundation walls are of brick, sitting on a foundation of concrete. These brick walls are only three bricks high. Sitting on top of these walls is galvanized metal RHS (one inch by one inch) square tube frame that the wire mesh is "Tec" screwed too.

The floor area to the open flights can be left natural or planted with lawn; this of course has to be maintained by either mowing or snipping that can be upsetting to nesting birds. I prefer to use river sand that is coarse, which allows water from heavy rain to drain away. The depth of this river sand should be at least six inches. Eclectus parrots do not often like to venture onto the ground. When they do they are nervous and the slightest noise sends them flying. I have found over the years that when they do spend time strutting about the ground they enjoy eating small amounts of the sand. This is most noticeable during nesting. Raking once a week easily cleans these river sand floors.

Eclectus parrots love to bathe so the installation of mist sprays on the roof of the open area of the flight is a must. On hot days twenty or thirty minute's morning and afternoon is ideal to keep these beautiful birds in top feather condition. A simple timer can be purchased for only a few dollars at the local hardware store; this saves water and time as it turns off the water if you are busy doing other things. When I was curator of birds at the Pearl Coast Zoological Gardens in Broome, Western Australia, I instructed our bird keepers to give all our birds twenty minutes morning and afternoon with the overhead mist sprays. This I believe contributed to the Zoo's breeding success of the Australian Eclectus Parrot *Eclectus roratus macgillivrayi*.

Other types of aviaries are suitable for breeding Eclectus parrots. Suspended aviaries are very popular here in Australia. These aviaries can be of an all wire mesh construction. The size varies but the best option is having at least a 12ft (3.6m) flight length. Using one inch by one inch by 1.6mm diameter weldmesh these suspended flights are 12ft long by 4ft. square (3.6m by 1.2m square). These wire mesh flights are then supported at a suitable height in rows of six to eight aviaries, with about eighteen inches between each flight. They are above the ground usually at a height that the front perch is at your eye level; they can be supported on galvanized pipe or rustic wooden posts. The shelter area can be accessed from inside a passageway or shed that also serves as a service area and feed store. The nest box is fixed to the inside wall of the service area with a hole cut into the shelter area and the open flight; nest boxes can be easily inspected without entering the shelter area.

The larger commercial breeders use portable-breeding aviaries for the breeding of Eclectus parrots, but mostly, these types of aviaries do not suit the private breeder because they require a more hands on daily routine of cleaning and feeding. The minimum size for this type of aviary is 12ft long by 3ft square (3.6m by 900mm. square), this style of breeding aviary is portable and is sometimes on wheels for easy movement indoors during bad weather. One end of this aviary is enclosed with sheet iron and the nest box is fixed to the outside. This style of aviary is constructed using one inch by one inch R.H.S. galvanized square metal tube either welded together or fixed using nylon molded corners. This aviary sits on a welded metal frame three feet above the ground and has three galvanized slide out metal trays for easy cleaning.

As breeders of these birds we would all like to have the best for our birds and if you have the space then consider a large planted aviary with multiple pairs of a particular sub species. The best planted aviary I have seen was at the Pearl Coast Zoological Gardens in Broome, Western Australia. It was here where I was working as Curator of Birds from 1986 to 1988 then as Director until 1993 that we had the opportunity to erect such an aviary. On one of his annual visits to his Zoo Lord Alistair McAlpine (The Lord McAlpine of West Green) was visiting from London. On one of our twice-daily walks around the zoo we discussed his plan for a large planted aviary. This aviary was to be a major exhibit for his zoo. He wanted a waterfall, running stream and planted with native trees and shrubs that were found in the species natural habitat.

Over the next few days we discussed what species would best suit this type of aviary. I had already had in the back of my mind that Eclectus parrots would be an excellent choice, Lord McAlpine was thinking about Macaws. I convinced him that due to the value of Macaws here in Australia they would be better suited to a single breeding aviary. He agreed, so it was agreed that the new aviary would house the New Guinea Eclectus Parrot *Eclectus roratus polychloros*.

As it was the norm with his Lordship there were no plans drawn up for this aviary, just a few sketches on a foolscap writing pad and scratches in the red "Pindan" desert sand of Broome to illustrate his ideas. After two weeks he would fly out and return to the U.K. On departure at the airport his last words would be "try and have it finished before I return" which would be in three months time. Then every day at precisely 3pm (7am London time) he would phone me for an update on the daily running of his zoo. And progress of the new aviary.

Thankfully Lord McAlpine had his own local building company in Broome restoring a number of the old pearling masters' homes as well as a number of other heritage buildings.

The size of this aviary was 150ft long by 50ft wide and 45ft high, (45m. long by 18m wide by 13.7m high); the building of this aviary was left to the supervisor of the building company under my supervision. One of my first tasks was to arrange the supply of the native plants; this was achieved with the help of the zoo's horticulturist and gardening staff. These native plants had to come from Perth, 2500 miles (4023km) to the south; we required truckloads of them, so a shadehouse had to be built to house these plants and acclimatize them. Full-grown palm trees were ordered and transplanted directly into their position in the aviary. Because Pandanus Palms *Pandanus spiralis* were native to the region that Eclectus parrots are found we wanted them to be the main feature in this aviary. I located a large stand of these palms on a cattle station about 50 miles (80km) to the east of Broome. Fortunately the owners of this station were good friends of Lord McAlpine. Permission was granted to remove a section of this stand of Pandanus palms and transported to the zoo.

Broome being a desert town, there were few large rocks that could be found locally that we could collect to construct the stream and waterfall that his Lordship wanted. These were found at the first mountain range 150miles (240km) to the north of Broome. I dispatched a crew, two trucks and a backhoe to collect them.

Three months later, Lord McAlpine was due; the aviary was nearing completion. At a cost of AU$250,000 and a lot of hard work by all the zoo staff it was ready to receive the birds.

Eight pairs of New Guinea Eclectus Parrots *Eclectus roratus polychloros* were selected and placed in holding cages inside the new aviary. A passive release method was to be used; this is where birds are not all released at the one time. Lord McAlpine phoned me the day before from Singapore to say he wanted to be present when the birds were released and would arrive the next day. The Lear Jet from Singapore touched down at 11am the next day; I met Lord McAlpine at the airport. He asked if everything was ready, I said yes. He said give me half an hour to get changed and I will see you at the zoo.

The eight pairs of Eclectus parrots were of various ages but nothing under two years of age. Only two pairs had produced before and these would be released last. When Lord McAlpine arrived he greeted his staff. Good morning, he said. Good morning, Alistair, the group of bird keepers replied. While in his zoo he wanted everything to be casual and instructed the staff to call him Alistair. He knew most of the staff by their first names; it was a very good working relationship. An hour earlier when I met him at the airport he was dressed in a dark pin striped suit looking the great businessman he was. But here at his zoo he was one of us, dressed in a well-worn pair of jeans, denim shirt and dusty Akubra hat and boots. Quite often visiting tourists would come up to me when Alistair was in the zoo, he and I and one or two keepers would be discussing future plans etc. when these tourists asked me if Lord McAlpine was in the zoo, not recognizing him standing there dressed so casually among us.

To observe the birds in this new large planted aviary we built an elevated wooden walkway and observation deck with steps leading up to almost tree top level. This observation deck also overlooked the waterfall and ponds that overfilled into the running stream. The roof of this observation deck was covered with palm fronds, which gave it a tropical effect. Seats were also provided.

The eight pairs of Eclectus parrots had been housed in holding cages for almost two days. It was now time to start releasing them. My plan was to release the four youngest males first, leave them an hour or so but with a keeper present to make sure that none of the birds hit the wire and injured themselves. Then the last four males were released, and we waited a further period of time. We observed that there was no fighting between any of the males. In fact they soon found the two feeding stations at either end of the aviary and spent most of the time flying high up and around the aviary. The four youngest females were then released and soon located their mates; this went so well that I decided to release the four older females. There was some squabbling over positions on perches but nothing violent.

The next morning I went to inspect the aviary very early, I wanted to be sure that they were all getting on okay together. Thankfully they all seemed extremely happy and excited about their new surroundings. The females would fly up and down the aviary just above the canopy of the pandanus palms followed by the males. I sat there for quite a while; the feeling I had was similar to the feeling I had years ago watching the Australian sub species in the wilds of Cape York.

Because of the height of this aviary the bird department and I came up with an idea for nesting positions within the aviary. We decided not to fix natural hollow logs or nest boxes to the wire mesh walls of the aviary because from the observation deck they would look out of place and too low in the tall aviary. We designed a galvanized telescopic pipe (one pipe inside another). The base pipe was 3inches (76mm) in diameter with a 2-3/4 inch (69mm) pipe inside it, the base pipe was set in concrete which left 10ft (3m) sitting upright. The internal pipe was 12ft (3.6m) long with a flat metal platform welded on the top. This platform was 1ft square (304mm) and was where the nest box was fixed.

The design of nest box I decided on was the "Grandfather Clock" style of nest. These were 2ft. high by 10 inches square (610mm. high by 254mm square) with an entrance hole near the top and a perch for the bird to land on. A weldmesh ladder made out of off cuts of 2x1inch by 2mm mesh were fixed to the inside of the front wall that contained the entrance hole, this allowed the female quick entry into her nest. An inspection door was fitted to one side of each nest, about 3inches (76mm) up from the bottom. The roof of the nest was 2inches (50mm) larger to prevent the nest filling with water during wet days. These nests were constructed out of waterproof marine ply half an inch thick (12mm).

Because of Broome's high daily temperature (28°C winter max. to 44°C summer max) I decided to provide ventilation holes around the top walls of each nest. This in time proved to be a great success in the summer months. When these nests were completed and fixed on top of these telescopic stands they could be raised up a various heights depending on where they were positioned within the aviary. Each nest then could be fixed at the required height by adjusting a handle welded into the top of the base pipe, this would fix and hold the nest very tight and there was not a lot of movement when fully extended. Twelve nests were erected for the eight pairs; this would prevent fighting over nest sites.

When the bird keeping staff did their weekly nest check it was a simple task to first check if the female was out of the nest then lower the nest down slowly to a level that made it easy to inspect. Then the nest was raised back to its original position. We bred many New Guinea Eclectus parrots in this aviary. Most of the babies were taken for hand rearing, any that were left to fledge were banded in the nest at three to four weeks so we could identify them and their parents.

When two of the pairs started to nest it was quite interesting to watch. The female would fly to a particular nest box followed by her mate. The female entered the nest and proceeded to scratch around, the male would either sit on the perch at the entrance to the nest or sit on top of it. If other males or females approached he would defend the nest by raising his wings and squawking loudly. When eggs were present in the nest the other pairs seem to respect their territory. If an unsuspecting young male happened to land on top of the nest the female inside would call out, and her mate would return and chase the young male off. There was not one case of injury or blood drawn by any of the pairs in this aviary.

A planted aviary with multiple pairs of Eclectus parrots should be considered as an excellent alternative to breeding any of the sub species of Eclectus parrots.

When keeping Eclectus parrots indoors as pets give them as large a cage as possible. Even better only let them use the cage to sleep in and return to when they are hungry. Eclectus parrots do not like to be confined in small spaces, they become noisy and aggressive and it's stressful to the bird and the owner. There are many beautiful ornate indoor aviaries available that are suitable for a pet Eclectus parrot. Some of these are on stands with wheels so they can be easily moved around. Position the indoor aviary near a window where it can get the morning sunlight and the bird has something to watch while you're away.

I knew an exotic parrot breeder that had a pair of New Guinea Eclectus parrots that he kept indoors, but never caged, they had free range of the living room. At one end of this living room there is a feature brick wall. On one end of this wall he fixed a natural dead tree branch where this pair of birds perched. There were food and water dishes fixed to this branch. At the other end of the brick wall he fixed a nest box, this was away from the end of the branch and they had to fly to reach it. This pair of Eclectus parrots was only about three years old and was hand reared and very tame. Each time the family sat down for their meals, down would fly the two birds and land on a special perch fixed to the top of a wooden chair. They were treated as part of the family, receiving food scraps and eating them on their perch. When finished they would fly up and return to their perch and sit and watch TV.

The female was spending a lot of time in the nest box, still too young to breed; it will be interesting when they do! Metal sand trays were provided on the floor under the nest box and perch to catch their droppings and any food scraps.

If living out of town on a large property or farm, then thought could be given to free flying Eclectus outdoors. I have **not** tried this myself but have heard that it has been tried on a few occasions with a great deal of success. I think that if I were going to try something like this I would like to make sure that they entered an aviary in the evening, to have peace of mind, that at least they were safe for the night.

Also before releasing a captive-bred bird into the wild I'd have to be sure of what predators were native to the area, and check with the local council to make sure that releasing non native species into the local environment, did not contravene the local council by laws.

Here in Australia, or at least one or two of our States, it's illegal to release captive bred birds (native or exotic) into the wild; this is mainly due to their possible pest potential. I had an unusual experience while I was in Broome Western Australia. One of our native birds (from another State) escaped, and I notified the officer of the local department of agriculture, which I'm required by law to do. He advised me that if we did not recapture it within 48 hours a special "flying squad" would be sent up from Perth (2500 miles away) to destroy the pest! And this could be at our cost. Thankfully the bird was recaptured the next day trying to get back inside its aviary. So it pays to check with the local council department first.

4.3 Diet for Eclectus Parrots

The single most important factor in the captive breeding and keeping of Eclectus parrots is their diet. These fascinating parrots are arboreal in habit; they frequent the uppermost canopy of fruit and blossom-laden trees high in open forest and tropical rainforest of Indonesia, Australia, Papua New Guinea and the Solomon Islands.

In captivity Eclectus parrots should be fed as close to their natural diet as possible. If we use a common sense approach to their daily

134

requirements and feed them a balanced fruit and vegetable diet they will remain in good health and feather.

If fed a seed only diet these birds become fat and lazy and will sit for long periods without moving. When they do move they prefer to climb around the wire instead of flying. These birds soon become non-breeders and may even start to feather pluck themselves. Birds that are forced to live this way do not live long and productive lives.

The daily diet and feeding routine that I use for my breeding pairs are as follows: for each singly housed pair, each morning they would get a six inch glazed earthenware bowl full of diced fruits, vegetables and cooked maize. I used a variety of fruits and these include apple, banana, pear, kiwi fruit, and grapes, vegetables such as green beans, snow peas, carrot, celery, and silver beet storks and washed lettuce or silver beet leaves.

In another bowl of the same size I would place a small handful of budgie breeders mix (Hungarian millet, Jap. Millet, Canary seed etc.). In the same bowl twice a week I would add a small sprinkling of grey sunflower seeds (feeding too much sunflower seed is not good for Eclectus parrots). My observations of Eclectus parrots in the wild is that they are all "lean and mean", as they spend most of their day flying from one feeding ground to another high above the canopy. To keep Eclectus parrots in this sort of condition we need to follow two rules: (1) do not over feed, and (2) they are fruit eaters and should be fed only very small amounts of seeds, Also Eclectus should not be fed pellets.

Preparing the fruit each morning, I would place into a two-gallon bucket a quantity of boiled maize that was cooked the day before, cooled and placed in the fridge overnight. This maize is washed before and after cooking. Into this bucket I added the diced fruit (bear in mind I had 70-odd birds to feed, so the amount of diced fruit was a large "Tupper ware" container full). The amount of dry maize that was to be cooked was a one-liter container full. By the time both the fruit and cooked maize were mixed together the two-gallon bucket was full.

About a cup of this fruit and maize mix is placed on a crisp lettuce leaf or silverbeet leaf, and when available chickweed was also used. Other green food such as dandelion (including the flowers and roots) were offered when available (usually in the winter months). Care should be taken to make sure that anything from the garden is thoroughly washed and free of pesticides, if there is any doubt then "throw it out."

The quantity of fruit and vegetables that was required to feed the number of birds I had was, six apples, three pears, four bananas, four kiwi fruit, two oranges, and a small bunch of grapes. (Each week the grapes would be changed, i.e. 1st week green, 2nd red and 3rd black) They prefer grapes with seeds. Vegetables would vary from day to day; the most often used were green beans, snow peas, raw carrot and silver beet storks. All the above fruit and vegetables would be diced or cut into small pieces and mixed into the cooked (soft) maize. No vitamins were added or fed to any of the adult pairs.

Special treat items such as guavas, pomegranates, passionfruit, rock melon, paw-paw and mango are fed when in season. Mangoes are especially welcomed, and they will spend days feeding and chewing on the seed. Other treats such as chilies, capsicum and celery are offered every now and then. Over the years that I have been keeping Eclectus parrots I have noticed that they prefer fruits that contain a lot of seeds. If fed a guava they will eagerly sit there cracking the seeds until only the skin is left; the same can be said for passionfruit.

Other foods like native fruits, nuts and berries are offered, such as sandpaper figs, *ficus opposita,* hawthorn berries, *crataegus monogyna* and *Pyracantha* berries; to supplement this fresh gum branches containing buds and blossoms are hung on the wall of the aviary.

I cannot stress enough the need to feed a balanced fruit and vegetable diet to all captive Eclectus parrots, be it a single much loved household pet or a pair or multiple breeding pairs. There is a saying here in

Australia "you only get out of them what you put in" and that's true when it comes to Eclectus parrots. If fed a proper balanced diet of the foods listed above, there will be no need to feed vitamins and additives to get the best out of your birds.

4.4 Nesting requirements

The nesting requirement for Eclectus parrots in captivity again comes down to personal choice. If you live on a large property or farm out in the country and there are plenty of natural hollow logs just lying around, you may decide to use them.

Many breeders new to keeping Eclectus parrots try to set them up in a reasonable size open flight with a natural hollow log hanging in the shelter section of the aviary. This is fine if you live here in Australia, close to state forest and have access plus a permit to remove these logs that lay on the floor of the forest. But those days are coming to an end; these logs are now being left for other forest animals, reptiles and insects and the wildlife authorities are asking us to leave them alone. This is fair enough; as breeders we should be more conservation conscious to other species that live in our forest.

If you live in a large city many bird shops and pet stores have a variety of hollow logs to choose from. They will also have a wide range of nest boxes. These will come at a cost and can be expensive. But unless you have a relative or a family friend that owns a property out of town, where you can find a suitable selection of natural logs, then you only have a couple of choices to make, (1) buy a hollow log or nest box from the pet store, or (2) make a nest box yourself.

When I first started keeping Eclectus parrots many years ago, I spent many hours out in the bush searching for just the right log. But I soon found once they started to breed and I wanted to inspect their nest, how difficult it was to see the eggs or chicks. I had to ward off a very aggressive hen that would delight in landing on the back of my neck and taking large chunks out of me.

When it came time to remove the two chicks for hand feeding, I had to catch both the adult birds and remove them to a holding cage. This was in my view very stressful, and I wanted to make the log more accessible. I decided to cut a 4inch (101mm) inspection door in the side of the log, I drilled four half inch holes and then cut a square hole using a jigsaw. I then fixed a couple of hinges and a barrel bolt to lock the door closed.

When this pair laid again I inspected the nest at least once a week. My aim was to get the breeding pair used to me opening the inspection door to the nest without upsetting them. This worked for a couple of weeks until the hen decided to dive into the nest the moment she saw me entering their aviary. There she would sit and as soon as I opened the door she proceeded to snap at my face or hand. It became a test of wits between us to see who would get to the chicks first, her or me.

It got to the stage that I had to first wait until the female was out of the nest and down the other end of the aviary. I would rush in and throw a towel over the entrance to the log, quickly do my inspection, remove the towel and leave the aviary.

The use of hollow logs for nesting in the aviary looks great if you are only keeping them as a hobby, and you let the parents rear their own young. But if you are a commercial breeder and have multiple breeding pairs then nest boxes would be the preferred option. Hollow logs may look good in the aviary and some of our pairs may prefer them. But they are hard to obtain; heavy to hang up in the aviary and you may need the use of chains to support them, which in turn can become obstacles for the birds to fly into.

Vermin present in an aviary will always set up house in a deep dark hollow log, and because of the weight of the log they are less likely to be removed for cleaning. When I was proprietor of a bird park back in the 70s I set most of our pairs of cockatoos and other species of parrots up with natural hollow logs. But due to some of the problems mentioned above I soon started to change to nest boxes. Another major problem we had living in far northern Queensland was pythons. These pythons ranged in size from 3ft (914mm) to 18ft. (5.4m), the smaller pythons were "children's pythons" and were harmless and fed mainly on mice and small birds. It was the larger "scrub pythons" that gave us the most heartache. During the long wet season from January to March they would enter the aviaries during the night. It became so bad I had to inspect every nesting log each morning before the gate was opened to the public, and in eight years I removed over 300 pythons from hollow logs.

Once I started using nest boxes the python problem started to ease. I think that the smell of a natural hollow log attracted the pythons as very few were found in the nest boxes.

One frightening experience I had that I will never forget was with a large Scrub Python *Morelia amethystina*. It was during the middle of the wet season and in the middle of the night, it had been pouring for hours, our house was at the rear of the park on top of a hill. I was woken by the screech of one of our blue and gold macaws. It was an erie cry for help. I bounded out of bed, threw on a pair of shorts, grabbed my rifle as I went out the door, and ran down the hill armed with a flashlight and rifle.

When I reached the aviary where the macaws were housed I was careful not to shine the torch directly on the birds. I checked the first aviary that housed the first pair of macaws, they were sitting asleep at the end of the perch, and all seemed quiet. I moved to the next aviary that housed the breeding pair of blue and gold macaws, and there was one of the birds still sitting on the perch with a huge python coiled around it, slowly crushing it. I fumbled for my keys and rushed around to the door that was on the other side of the first aviary. As I entered I realized that in my haste to get down the hill as quickly as I could I forgot to grab the magazine containing the bullets for the rifle.

I tried not to disturb the first pair of macaws, who were still sleeping and did not hear me enter due to the heavy rain. I reached the inner door, and slowly opened it to find the macaw and python rolling on the ground. My first thought was to shoot the python, but no bullets! So I used the rifle as a club and hit the python as hard as I could. The poor macaw had just about given up the ghost. I struck the python hard again, and finally it tried to get away and started to uncoil itself from the macaw. I was more worried about the bird than the python. As I was trying to help the macaw back up onto its perch the python disappeared into the night.

At daylight the next morning I was surprised to find both the blue and golds flying up and down their aviary as if nothing had happened. Where was the python? There were two large hollow logs and one large nest box in the two aviaries. I looked in the nest box first, but it was empty. I then checked the larger of the two logs thinking that if I were a python with a headache this is where I would hide. It too was empty. I was not sure of the size of this python because I was more interested in getting it free from the macaw.

The last log was the smaller of the two and I was sure it was too small for this python. The gate to the park had just opened and our first tourist coach had just arrived. I quickly put the rifle (plus bullets this time) out of sight; no need to frighten the tourists. I started to climb up the wire to look inside the log when a visitor asked me if I was looking for eggs. I said no, not quite, I then looked into this log and there within about five inches from my face was this huge python, with fright I fell back, much to the delight of the small crowd of tourists that had gathered to watch what I was doing.

I said something that can't be repeated here, but somewhere in the few words I did say was "snake." So I now had a crowd that wouldn't leave until I removed the python. I decided to get a stepladder and lower the log down to the ground and prod the python out with a stick. The log fell to the ground and out came the python. This snake I thought was big, but not this big. It measured just under eighteen feet (5.4 meters) long. The macaws seeing the python went berserk and were flying up and down the aviary. I had to remove it quickly and with the public present I wasn't about to shoot it.

One of my birdkeepers was close by, so I called him over to give me a hand. As he entered the aviary I pounced on the python grabbing it by the neck, it instinctively started to coil around me. This python was at least six inches thick. I could just get my hands around the neck. Luckily for me I had some experience with these large pythons. I encountered many on my bird watching and collecting trips in the rainforests of Cape York. As long as you don't let it lock its tail you have a good chance of capturing it. Peter my birdkeeper had hold of its tail. I said be sure you don't let it go. We struggled with it until we were out of the aviary and a member of the public helped us place it in a sack.

The excitement was over so the group of tourists moved onto the next exhibit all excited with the experience they just had. They all certainly got their money's worth that day. A few days later I released the python into the rainforest up on the Atherton Tableland west of Cairns about 48km (30miles) away.

Deciding that nest boxes would be better suited for my captive-breeding programs, I looked through my diaries of the expeditions that I had done to Cape York over the past five years. Out of the entire Australian Eclectus parrots nest that were inspected the highest percentage was at an average depth of between three and four feet (914 mm and 1.2 meters) deep.

The size nest box required for the Australian Eclectus parrot *Eclectus roratus macgillivrayi,* this being the largest sub species, was 36 inches high by 14 inches square (914mm high by 355mm square) using half-inch (12mm) thick waterproof marine ply. The style of this nest was the "grandfather clock" style that was fixed in an upright position in the aviary.

A six-inch diameter entrance hole was cut in two inches below the roof of the nest. With a six inch perch fitted a further four inches below the entrance hole, this allowed the male to perch at the entrance and look in and watch over his mate. He also fed the female from this perch. An inspection door six inches square was cut into the side closest to the service entrance door of the aviary. This allowed for quick access for nest inspection or chick removal.

An internal heavy gauge 2x1-inch wire mesh ladder was fitted to the front wall just below the nest entrance hole. This has to be fixed securely and had to reach to the top of the nesting material. It also assisted the female entering and leaving the nest, and it also prevented the female jumping in and damaging the eggs. When the nest boxes were completed they were painted with an acrylic mission brown fence dressing and allowed to dry for at least three days before use. This paint is non toxic.

This size nest box would be suitable for the Grand Eclectus *Eclectus roratus roratus,* the Vosmaeri Eclectus *Eclectus roratus vosmaeri,* the Aru Island Eclectus *Eclectus roratus aruensis,* and the Cornelia Eclectus *Eclectus roratus cornelia.* For the smaller sub species i.e. the Red Sided Eclectus *Eclectus roratus polychloros,* the Solomon Island Eclectus *Eclectus roratus solomonensis*, the Biak Island Eclectus *Eclectus roratus biaki,* the Tanimbar Island Eclectus *Eclectus roratus riedeli.* The suitable nest box size would be 24 inches high by 10 inches square (609 mm. high by 254 mm. square) and in the same style and design as for the larger sub species.

Deciding what type of nesting material to use is as important as deciding what diet we feed our breeding pairs. To me personally it's an extremely important part of successfully breeding these magnificent birds. Over the years I have tried many different types of nesting material from sawdust to leaf mulch and a lot of things in between.

Many breeders choose to use dry wood shavings for nesting material, probably because it's clean and easy to obtain. In my opinion it's too dry and does not provide enough moisture, which in turn builds up the humidity inside the nest box which provides for better egg development and hatching.

When I had the chance to inspect Eclectus parrots' nests in the rainforest of far northern Australia, I was a little surprised to find the majority of them to be quite moist and in a few cases wet! So wet that if you squeezed a handful of the nesting material in your hand water would drip out. When I finally started breeding the Australian sub species I had a much better hatching success using damp or moist nesting material.

Before I bred my first Eclectus parrots I was living in Sydney and specializing in the Australian black cockatoos. For all my nests (which were natural logs at the time) I used natural wood dust. This wood dust was found inside dead hollow logs lying on the floor of the national park that bordered my property in Sydney. On Sundays my family and I would spend the day looking for hollow logs and nesting material, I would take with me some hessian bags and when a suitable log was found we would scrape out the wood dust into these bags.

This type of nesting material I used for many years and it's still one of the best materials to use today. If I required it a little moister I would empty a bag of this wood dust onto a concrete slab and sprinkle it with water and mix it like you would cement. I often added fresh gum leaves to the mix which I thought would help keep out mites and insects. It also made the nest smell fresh and natural.

In the early 1980s I experimented with live termite mounds. These mounds are found on the ground in the forest and can be from just a few inches high to six or seven feet high. The ones I preferred were between one and two feet high because they were easier for me to lift and place in the back of my vehicle. How I came to use these termite mounds was purely by accident. I was keeping two Australian mound nesting parrots at the time the Hooded Parrot *Psephotus dissimilis* and the Golden-shouldered Parrot *Psephotus chrysopterygius*. I wanted to provide a natural nesting environment for them. In the wild these parrots would only nest in live mounds that contained termites. I cemented the base of the mound to stop the termites leaving and placed it on top of a metal frame. The legs of this frame were placed in water to stop any termites that tried to escape the mound.

Within days both pairs of parrots started to excavate a tunnel and soon nested. When the breeding season was over I removed these mounds and replaced them the following season with new ones. I was then faced with the problem of what to do with the old termite mounds; I proceeded to break them up in a wheelbarrow. The termites had died during the months they laid dormant as nests in the aviary. Once these mounds were broken up I realized I had what I thought was good looking nesting material. I decided to try it in the nests of my Eclectus parrots. The first pairs I tried it with seemed to enjoy getting down and scratching in it, as well as eating it. I would break the mounds up into reasonably small pieces, about ¾ of an inch to an inch in size. I would occasionally leave a larger piece on top of the fresh nesting material for the female to chew up.

When I took up the position of curator of birds at the zoo in Broome, Western Australia in 1986 I continued to use crushed termite mounds as nesting material. We also tried other materials such as freshly cut coconut palm fronds and eucalyptus branches and leaves; these were put through a mulcher by our gardening department and stored in large plastic bins. Both these types of nesting materials worked well in the hot desert climate of the Kimberleys.

Since moving back to the east coast of New South Wales in 1993 and specializing in Eclectus parrots I continued using the termite mounds for my nesting material. Thankfully supply of termite material was not a problem because my friend and neighbor Graham Bradley was one of the leading finch breeders in the State. Graham would spend days collecting termite mounds up and down the coast. He wanted the mounds not for nesting material, but for the live termites found inside, each week he would break up these mounds into large pieces and place them into a tumbling machine he designed and built.

This machine extracted the live termites, which he fed out to his large collection of native and foreign finches. The residue from the tumbling machine now free of termites was placed into empty seed bags and stored.

The use of termite mounds for nesting material is still my preferred choice as the best for most species of parrots and cockatoos.

After losing chicks with wood chips lodged in their crops, I decided to try the crushed termite mound as the base in the brooders. As most breeders of Eclectus parrots would know having a chick with a piece of wood lodged in the crop is a worrying time. You only have one or two options, (1) when the chick's crop is about half full turn the chick upside down and try and force the food and the piece of wood back up and out of the mouth. This can be very upsetting for the chick and in some cases fatal; (2) take the chick to a qualified avian veterinarian and have it surgically removed— this also is very stressful for the chick and in some cases they do not survive the surgery.

When I changed over to using the termite nesting material in my brooders I found that when a chick was placed back in the brooder after being fed, it would continue pumping for food and would lay flat on the termite material. If a small piece of material entered its beak the chick would think it was food and swallow it. The next time this chick was due for feeding, its crop was felt and several small pieces of termite mound were in the bottom of the crop. I just left these small pieces and continued feeding the chick. I placed this chick in an ice cream container with paper towels as a base, this way I could monitor its droppings. The next morning this chick was empty and no pieces of termite mound were felt in the crop. Its droppings indicated that the entire termite mound had dissolved and had passed safely through.

This is why I firmly believe that the use of materials such as termite mound is much safer than wood shavings or wood chips as nesting and brooder material for Eclectus parrots. It is also possible that by using termite mound as nesting material the Eclectus parrots may be getting hidden benefits such as vitamin and minerals left behind by the termites.

Materials that are not recommended for nesting material are "peat moss." and materials such as commercial potting mixes and mulch that is commercially prepared and sold through nursery outlets. Many of these mixtures contain added chemicals and fertilizers. If materials such as these are used in nests and the female begins scratching the fine dust she kicks up can be quite harmful if ingested through the bird' nostrils.

4.5 Catching and moving

When there is a need to catch and relocate Eclectus parrots from one enclosure to another, it's important to have the proper equipment to do this, so it is carried out quickly and without unnecessary stress or injury to the bird.

Before deciding to catch a bird that you are moving to another aviary some distance away, it's important to have a suitable carrying box ready for this task. Having a pair of soft cotton gloves and a suitable size catching net is also necessary.

Because I handle a lot of birds I prefer to use gloves. Some breeders use only their bare hands— this in my opinion is much more harmful to the birds because you tend to hold them tighter, hoping not to get bitten. Some breeders think it's a "macho" thing and think it makes them look good if they can catch the bird using only their hands. The same can be said about catching birds without the use of a net. I can recall a few times that I have called into purchase birds from breeders that are fairly new to aviculture, to be amazed at how unprepared they were. One bloke went in with a towel and spent at least fifteen minutes chasing this pair of birds around this quite large aviary. When he finally caught the male he held it so tight I had to say sorry but I'm not interested now because the bird is so stressed.

He lost a sale and could have also lost one or both of his birds. Another experience I had that stuck in my mind was to do with the incorrect use of a bird net. I was living in Sydney at the time and was breeding Australian black cockatoos. I read in the Saturday paper that a breeder had a pair of Gang Gang Cockatoos *Callocephalon fimbriatum* for sale. So I phoned him and made a time for the next day to come out and look at them. I arrived and introduced myself. He then showed me around his birds. The size of these aviaries was amazing; they were about 10foot high and at least 35 to 40ft long (3.4m high and at least 10.6m to 12m long).

I was shown the pair of Gang Gangs. They were a nice young pair. I said I would take them and returned to collect my carrying box from my vehicle. When I returned he was waiting for me with his catching net. We entered the rear of the aviary and he proceeded to catch these birds. There were other birds in this aviary at the time and as I watched him trying to net these birds, I was astounded to see him swishing the net as if he was playing tennis, not letting the birds fly past, then quickly placing the net in front of the bird he is trying to catch. After a few minutes I asked him if he would mind if I caught them, as I did not want them over stressed. He agreed and in fact I think he was glad that I had offered. While I was catching the two birds I demonstrated to him the best way to net birds in an aviary this size. He appreciated my help; not too many would, and even get offended at the mere suggestion that they do not know how to catch birds correctly.

The best way to catch birds in an aviary situation is first have the right size net. The size net I prefer is a 12 inch (304mm.) round one, with a ¾ inch mesh size, and only 18 inches (457mm.) deep. The rim of the net is lightly padded, and the overall length (from the top of the net to the end of the handle) is just 2 ft. six inches (762mm.) long. This size net is suitable for most aviaries and suspended aviary conditions. The proper way to catch birds in this type of net is to first practice with catching things in it. And the only way I can describe this is first you need two other people, get them to stand about ten feet apart and pass a tennis ball between them. With yourself standing in between them, they should not throw the ball hard, just fast enough for you to reach out and scoop the ball as it passes by you. After a bit of practice you learn to lead the ball with the net and the ball falls in. Then it's time to practice on the real thing. Start with a bird that is easy to catch and not one of your more valuable ones. If you have practiced it well, nothing will hurt the bird. Soon you will be confident enough to catch anything.

Now you have caught the bird properly, do you know how to hold it correctly and remove it from the net? As mentioned earlier, I prefer to use cotton gloves to handle birds, in fact I use two pairs of these cotton gloves, "one pair inside the other"; this gives the bird something to bite instead of your finger, and the double thickness does not hamper your grip on the bird.

If you are right handed then you hold the bird with your left hand, leaving your right hand free to open the door to the carrying box, attach leg bands and so on. When reaching into the net (which now should be on the ground) slowly try and get your thumb on the birds right hand side (the bird should be facing away from you) of its head. Your first index finger should be on the other (left-hand) side of the bird's head, the palm of your hand and the rest of your fingers hold the bird's wings closed against its body. This is the correct way to hold birds, with both your thumb and forefinger preventing the bird from biting. If it does manage to latch onto either your thumb or forefinger it will only bite into the double layer of cotton gloves.

It surprises me how many breeders of parrots and cockatoos do not know the correct way, first to catch the bird safely in the net, and secondly when they catch it, they have no idea of how to hold it. I remember many years ago a well known breeder here in Australia that kept cockatoos. I was visiting with a friend, who wanted to pick up a pair of Long-billed Corellas *Cacatua tenuirostris*. When my friend had decided on which pair of birds he wanted the owner went inside his shed and returned wearing these thick leather gloves. My mate and I looked at each other, thinking, "What does he need those for?" He also had a huge net, similar to what you use when fishing in a boat. The net was at least four feet deep and the frame was metal and unpadded.

When he managed to finally catch one of the long-bills, the bird was bleeding from just above the cere; it was quite obvious that this bird had been hit across the head by the metal part of the net. But that was not the worst of it. When he tried to remove the cockatoo from the net, he grabbed it by the tip of the wings and folded them back together holding both tips, with the cockatoo hanging below. He then proceeded to poke the head of the bird into the carrying box. By the time both birds were caught and were in the carrying box they looked a mess, both were spotted with blood and looked much stressed out. He threw a towel over them and calmly said they would be okay by the time we got them home.

My friend and I walked away to discuss what we should do. I said there was no way I would accept these birds and recommended that my friend do the same. My friend had known this man for a long time and did not want to offend him; he decided, when the owner of the birds guaranteed that if either of the birds died, he would replace it or refund the money, he decided that he would accept them. This could have been all avoided if the owner had some idea of catching and holding the birds that he had in his care.

There was no need for thick leather gloves or such a large net. If a net is too deep, you then run the risk of a fast flying bird (such as a lorikeet or lory) breaking its neck when it hits the side of the net before it reaches the bottom. The net length should be only long enough that you can fold it over with the bird inside, this safely holds the bird until you remove it. In my opinion the depth of the net should be between 18 inches and two feet deep (457mm and 610mm deep), the mesh size should be around ¾ of an inch (19mm) and not too thick, to allow for light and easy movement through the air.

The use of leather gloves of any sort should be avoided due to lack of feeling when holding a bird. Most people tend to hold the bird too tightly because they can't feel it properly, and in some cases they don't hold the bird tight enough and the bird escapes. The cotton gardening gloves I prefer to use are available from most department stores, both here and overseas, and can be purchased for only a few dollars.

Eclectus parrots can inflict nasty bites if not caught and held properly. They are very intelligent birds and know when they are about to be caught. With my own birds, the moment I step out of my garage holding my bird net the word spreads from aviary to aviary— even the birds that cannot see me know I'm coming to catch one of them. It then becomes a battle of wits to try and not get caught. The only ones that are not sure what's going on are young recently fledged Eclectus, usually young males, they just sit there and you can put the net over their head, while still sitting on their perch. But the very next time you go to catch them it's a much different story.

Chapter 5
The Removal of Chicks, and Handfeeding

What is the best age to remove young Eclectus parrot chicks from the nest for hand rearing? The answer to this question will depend on what type of Eclectus parrot breeder you are. If you are a hobbyist and keep Eclectus parrots and other species of parrots purely for the enjoyment of watching these magnificent birds fly in a large aviary, and you are only interested in them breeding if they want to, then I would not remove the chicks but let the parents rear them. There is a great deal to learn and enjoy, plus it's a great feeling of satisfaction in watching young birds leave the nest for the first time.

On the other hand if you are breeding birds for a living or have a large collection of parrots, or if there is a need to supplement your income, then removing chicks from the nest is the most effective way to achieve this. Eclectus parrots are among the few species of parrots that are regular repeat breeders. If you live in the right climate, it's then possible to breed your Eclectus all year round (although only five to six clutches per year is recommended). Then give them a spell. Most breeding pairs of Eclectus parrots will repeat another clutch within ten to twenty days after the removal of chicks, or if eggs are removed for artificial incubation.

5.1 When to remove them

The best age to remove young Eclectus parrot chicks from the nest is between ten and fourteen days of age. If removed at this age they have received the best possible start in life from the parent birds. At this age they can be placed in the brooder. If removed chicks are less than ten days of age they will require being kept in an intensive care unit and monitored more frequently with the temperature and humidity strictly controlled.

When a decision has been made to remove a brood of chicks the first thing to do is to be prepared to place them in the brooder. The brooder must be operating for at least 24 hours before the first chicks are placed inside it. Check and note the changes in temperature and be sure you have the plastic holding containers washed and ready with clean nesting material or paper towels inside. When it's time to remove the chicks it's important not to rush it, but be sure in the approach you are taking. Most, if not all, female Eclectus parrots are aggressive when they are at nest, so it's important not to first go and have a look then decide that you will take them. The adult female will know that you plan to take her chicks and will be ready for you, usually sitting behind the inspection door between you and her two chicks. If proper records are kept (I use a simple calendar) and you mark the date the first egg was laid and then when the second egg was laid you can calculate a hatch date (28days from the date the second egg was laid) give or take a day. Then count forward 10 or 14 days and mark this date as your chick removal date.

I only do weekly nest checks. Some breeders prefer to check every day; I feel that checking too often tends to make the breeding pairs much more aggressive.

When the chicks have been transferred to the brooder, check each chick all over, count the number of toes making sure that none are constricted or have any bite marks that may require treatment. Check the beak, the eyes and last of all check the crop to see how much food is there and determine when the first feed will be. Recently removed chicks should not be fed until the crop is empty.

On transferring the first clutch of chicks to the brooder it's important to keep a written record of the details for each bird. I use a card file and record such details as the parents' identification number or leg band numbers, the aviary number that the chicks came from plus any details of the chick's first inspection should be recorded. If the chicks are only ten to fourteen days old it will be difficult to tell their sex. In time with a trained eye you will be able to determine their sex at this age due to the shade of gray down (usually the female is a darker steel gray and the male a paler silver gray). Also you will develop a "feel" for their manner. Males are more outgoing and are inquisitive of their surroundings, where young females tend to sit and be shy!

I do not leg band my chicks until they have "broken color," which is when they are around four weeks of age. Color first appears around the ears and then the crown of their heads. Once they have broken color I leg band them and add their ID. Numbers to their record cards. Until they have broken color they are kept in plastic ice cream containers in individual clutches. I write on each container the number of the aviary they came from by using a felt pen. Once all the chicks contained in the brooder have been leg banded I take them out of the plastic containers and let them mix and socialize with each other. At this time it's important to keep a close eye on them because some of the slightly older birds tend to pick on the smaller ones. This only lasts a few hours; soon they should all be nest buddies.

5.2 Brooders

There are a variety of brooders available on the market today; it's important to choose the one that best suits your own situation. The one I use and found to be the most reliable is one I designed and built myself.

Commercially made brooders can range in price from a few hundred dollars to a thousand dollars or so. All of them are suitable for raising young Eclectus parrot chicks. There are a couple of things to consider before you purchase a brooder: (1) that the unit is easy to clean, (2) that it has a reliable heating unit, one that can be easily obtained and replaced. Some units come with a circulating fan that keeps the warm air moving and circulates fresh air. Humidity is also important in the brooder, at least for the first few weeks. Once chicks are six to eight weeks of age the humidity is not so important. Humidity helps with feather development and softens the feather sheaths to allow for quicker feather growth. Once the young Eclectus parrot chicks have been leg banded and grouped together I remove the humidity water tray, as they no longer require it. They receive enough moisture/humidity from their droppings. Fresh nesting material (crushed termite mound) is replaced every few days, depending on the number of chicks in each brooder.

The size of the brooders that I built and use are 20inches square by 15inches deep (508mm square by 381mm deep), with a hinged lift up lid to the top of the box. It is constructed using ½ inch marine ply that is painted with a non-toxic acrylic paint. Four light globe sockets are fixed to the inside bottom of the brooder, one in each corner, the electrical wires that feed these sockets are covered inside plastic conduit and attached to the bottom of the inside of the brooder. All four wires are attached to a Honeywell wall thermostat that is fitted two thirds of the way up on the front inside wall of the brooder (high enough that chicks can not reach it). A dimmer control switch is fitted on the outside of the brooder, back to back with the thermostat. This switch also contains a light that glows when the thermostat clicks on, it also controls the brightness of the light globes. Only use low wattage bulbs no higher than **40watt.** If brighter and hotter bulbs are used it may cause damage to young birds' eyes.

Do not use clear or pearl globes, as these are too bright. Only use colored bulbs. I recommend yellow, green or blue globes, as these when used with the dimmer control give off plenty of warmth and enough light not to disturb the young birds. Each globe and light socket is enclosed inside a ½ by ½ inch wire mesh screen so the birds cannot touch the bulbs. The nesting material hides the plastic conduit containing the electrical wiring, which is at least 3inches deep.

Ventilation holes are drilled in each wall of the brooder, two ¼ inch holes per side, one at a level just above the top of the nesting material on the left-hand side of the wall. The other hole is two inches from the top of the box on the right hand side of the wall; this permits airflow and as hot air rises it exits the brooder from the top holes. This type of brooder does not require a fan. Lifting the lid expels enough air to refresh the brooder.

At least two brooders are necessary, even for the casual breeder. You need the second one operating or at least ready when it's time to clean the first one. This way it's an easy task to just transfer the chicks from one brooder to the other. I have between three and four brooders ready at any one time, and depending on the season and the age of the chicks two or three will contain chicks of various ages. When a brooder is cleaned I like to sit it out in the sunlight for a few hours, just to make sure it's clean and dry.

The temperature in the brooder will depend on the age of the chicks you are placing inside it, e.g. if the brooder has no chicks already in it and the first clutch of chicks are fourteen days old then the temperature should be set at 86° degrees Fahrenheit (30°C). When a clutch has been placed inside the brooder for the first time, leave the lid of the brooder closed for 30 minutes, then recheck the temperature and adjust if necessary.

If the brooder already contains older chicks then the temperature should be read and adjusted upwards to the required reading. Older chicks will adjust to a slightly higher temperature better that the younger ones adapting to a lower one. You will find that once there is a number of various size chicks in the brooder it will be much easier to regulate, due to their combined body heat.

I find that the two-liter plastic ice cream containers are the best to use in the brooder. They are just the right size to fit a number of them in the brooder and they hold two Eclectus chicks comfortably until they outgrow them, which is then time to group them together. These containers should be washed and be ready for use. They should be cleaned and fresh nesting material or paper towels replaced every couple of days. It is also advisable to drill two ventilation holes in each side of these plastic containers to allow warm air to circulate.

5.3 The Intensive Care Unit

If there is a need to remove chicks that are under ten days of age, then these chicks will need to be housed in an Intensive care unit. Chicks of this age will require a higher temperature setting; the diet will also need to be adjusted for these younger birds.

Again there are many good quality intensive care units available on the market today. The ones we used in the bird department at the Pearl Coast Zoological Gardens, Broome, were imported from the United States. These were the Animal Intensive Care Units designed by Hannis L. Stoddard D.V.M. These clear and white acrylic units were light and weighed 28lbs (12.7 kg.). They were easy to clean, because the heating unit and fan were enclosed in a separate compartment and could be removed by removing just two screws. This then enabled the entire unit to be placed into a large plastic tray for washing and disinfecting.

The size of these units were 32 inches by 14 and a half inches by 13 inches deep (812mm.x 355mm.x330mm. deep). The clear plastic sliding doors and lift up lid made for easy inspection of small chicks, which could be observed without opening the unit, as the unnecessary opening of these doors will drop the temperature within the unit. This unit comes with a removable water tray, which is filled from a separate door on the front of the heater/fan compartment. This water tray is important to maintain humidity within the unit.

Over the years these units produced many healthy Eclectus parrot chicks. The only problem we had with them was (1) the digital read out display which gave out the temperature reading within the unit would differ to a thermometer reading where the chicks were situated.

This was overcome by placing two extra thermometers, one fixed on the inside of the front wall (just above the height of the chicks) and the other fixed to the rear wall. These were used to read the temperature where the chicks were. The digital read out display was one or two degrees higher. (2) The only other problem we had with these units was the electric fan would fail about every six months or so and had to be replaced. These were easy to obtain, as they were the same fans used in computers. Extra fans were always kept on hand and only took five minutes to change over.

Although many Eclectus parrot breeders prefer not to remove chicks that are under ten days of age, there will come a time when the need arises, e.g. the adult female or male dies, escapes or becomes ill. There are many unforeseen reasons why you will need an intensive care unit. If you are a breeder that prefers to remove fertile eggs for artificial incubation, then this type of intensive care unit will be a must for your bird nursery.

The temperature required for chicks that are under ten days of age will depend on what age the chicks are at the time of their removal. The rule of thumb temperature is calculated as follows: if the egg incubation temperature is 99.5°F (37.4°C.) and the age of the chicks is only one day old then the intensive care unit temperature should be set at 98.5°F (36.5°C.). Care should be taken once chicks are placed in the intensive care unit to monitor their progress. Make sure that after 30minutes the chicks are not overheating or too cold. The chicks should be a nice pink in color and feel warm to touch. If they are cold to touch or look pale in color then the temperature will have to be adjusted up slightly.

Eclectus parrot chicks at this age should be placed in small plastic containers that are lined with soft paper towels. I use clear round plastic containers, the type you get at the Chinese take away restaurant. These when washed are ideal to use in the intensive care unit, they are not too high and do not easily tip over. Eclectus parrot chicks at this age cannot support themselves even if there are two chicks, they will roll over backwards and lay on their backs. It's important to support these chicks either with a soft cloth or soft paper towels. I also use a small soft fluffy toy (teddy bear), the type that can be washed. This gives the small chicks something to snuggle up to.

By using the method described above and providing you have kept a record of their hatch dates, it then will be possible to calculate their age and then to work out the correct temperature each batch of chicks would require in the intensive care unit. Allowing a drop of a half a degree F or so per day of age will give you a starting point to achieve this.

The humidity inside the intensive care unit does not need to be as high as in the incubator. I usually fill the removable water tray about one quarter full and check and refill to that level each evening. Do not let the water tray completely dry out for any length of time, as the chicks will quickly dehydrate. Alternatively do not over fill the water tray, as this will cause moisture to collect on the inside walls and create a damp atmosphere within the unit.

The diet for chicks that are under ten days of age should be a lot thinner in consistency. This can be achieved by either straining the mixture that is prepared for older Eclectus parrot chicks, or by adding a little extra water. Or mix one level teaspoon of Ensure® (Abbott Laboratories, U.S.A.) infant formula to two teaspoons of boiled water, feed this every three hours for the first three days (this diet is only for chicks that are three days old or less). The temperature of the formula for feeding Eclectus parrot chicks should be kept at between 102°F and 105°F (38.9°C and 40.6°C). To maintain the temperature of the formula while feeding a clutch of chicks I stand the container holding the formula in a dish of hot water, I place a thermometer in the mixture and read it constantly during the hand feeding process. The best type of thermometer I have found for this task is the one butchers use to poke into meat to read the temperature. These are metal and have a round easy to read dial (similar to a wrist watch face) and can be checked at a glance. If the formula is above 105°F then I remove it from the hot water and let it stand for a while. Chicks should not be fed formula higher in temperature than 105°F.

Once chicks are ten days old their diet is changed to the diet that is fed to the older chicks. At this age they are also transferred from the intensive care unit to the brooder. When chicks at this age are transferred to the brooder the temperature should be set at 86°F (30°C). This is providing that they are the only chicks in this brooder. If the brooder contains chicks that are older then care should be taken that the older birds do not tip over the container holding the younger birds. This is one of the main reasons to have more than one brooder set up and operating in the bird room, as this allows for the keeping batches of chicks in age groups and prevents overcrowding.

The intensive care unit should be wiped out every day with a mild disinfectant cloth. Be sure to remove any small specks of food that may have been thrown out of the chicks' beaks and has stuck to the sides or floor of the plastic containers or even the walls of the unit. The entire unit should be thoroughly washed and disinfected at least once a week and wiped dry. The bedding material used in the plastic containers should be replaced each morning during their first feed for the day. This bedding material should be examined to check the droppings of the previous night; this will be the first place you will notice if anything is amiss, either with the formula or the operating temperature. The formula may have been too thick and will need to be thinner, or the temperature was too low and will require adjustment.

Eclectus parrot chicks at this age are fed every three hours or when their crops are empty. When they are transferred to the brooder they are fed every four hours. The first feed is at 7am then 11am, 3pm, 7pm and their last feed just before I go to bed, usually around 11.30pm. Chicks do not require feeding in the early hours of the morning. I find that this helps the chicks to digest and pass all the food by morning and makes them a lot more eager to be fed at their 7am feed.

I receive many phone calls from breeders that are new to aviculture that are worried about their chicks during the night. Especially during the first few days of age, "should I get up and feed them through the night," I'm asked. My standard answer to this question is remember that the crop is a storage area and when this area is empty there is still plenty of food in their system. Food travels through the crop into the proventriculus, gizzard and stomach and takes a few hours before the chick would be completely empty. By the time the 7am feed comes around the chick is active and hungry and is eager for food.

After each chick has been fed it's important to clean around the chick's beak including inside the bird's mouth. I use a soft damp tissue (toilet roll as these are just the right size) to wipe the outside of their beaks. I then use a moistened cotton bud to swab the inside of the mouth and around the tongue. Be careful when using the common type of cotton bud as they tend to come apart at times and can cause problems if swallowed by the chick. I use the longer type that are available from your local avian veterinarian. These are easier to manage and do not fray during use. Only use each cotton bud the once and do not use it on any other chicks; throw it away when finished. All feeding utensils should be thoroughly washed between feeds. Formula that is prepared in the morning should be stored in the fridge and discarded after the 11.30pm feed. I prefer to make a fresh batch of formula for each feed; this way I reduce the chance of chicks becoming infected from bacteria from unused formula.

If any of the chicks housed in the intensive care unit or in the brooders becomes ill, e.g. if a chick still has food in its crop at the 7am feed, or a chick keeps bringing up its food by regurgitation, then it's important to isolate this chick from others within the ICU or brooder. The chick that still has food in the crop at the 7am feeding time may not be ill and may just have a slow crop or because the mixture was a little too thick the night before. A little warm water should be fed to this chick and the crop gently massaged and left and checked in an hour. If the food does not pass by the time its due for its next feed then contact your local avian veterinarian for their advice.

A chick that throws up its food moments after being fed could only mean that it was overfed. A chick that throws up its food after an hour or so could mean there is an infection in its crop and will require treatment. Contact your avian veterinarian again for advice and treatment. The most common illness that affects young Eclectus parrots during the hand feeding process is sour crop. Sour crop if not treated soon develops into *Candida albicans*; this is a yeast like fungal infection of the mouth and crop. This illness called candidiasis is treatable using the drug Nystatin; it is available over the counter at your local pharmacy and is used in the treatment of thrush in babies.

The isolation of any chick that is infected with candidiasis is extremely important. If it is not isolated it will quickly infect the other chicks in the brooder. Contact your local avian veterinarian to take a swab of the infected chick's mouth. He then can determine if *Candida albicans* is present and then prescribe treatment. The infected chick will need to be kept isolated for the course of this treatment, usually seven days. Care should be taken to remove all the plastic containers and bedding material from the brooder that contained the infected bird; these containers should be disinfected and washed thoroughly. The inside walls should also be washed to remove any specks of food that may have come from the infected chick's mouth. Candidiasis is highly contagious and all feeding utensils should be disinfected and washed, including your hands.

As a matter of practice any chick that has a suspected infection is always fed last. This at least will ensure that transmission of any infection is minimized.

5.4 Hand Feeding

For me, the hand feeding of Eclectus parrot chicks is one of the most enjoyable tasks in aviculture. Whether you're feeding one or a dozen, to me they are such a delight to care for. Each chick will soon develop its own personality, even chicks that are only a few days old soon become identifiable by their own individual traits. And as soon as their eyes open they soon start to recognize who you are as they already know you by the sound of your voice.

Eclectus parrots are very intelligent birds and soon discover just by that sound of your voice that you bear them no harm. I talk to all my chicks from the moment they hatch in the incubator or from the first moment they are removed from the nest. This is irrespective of whether or not they are intended as future breeders or sold as pets; they all receive the same degree of chatter from me.

By talking to your chicks during feeding times helps the chicks (and yourself) to relax and enjoy the moment. Until these chicks that I am hand rearing have broken color they are all called "Ark wark." This I derived over the years from their calls in the wild. It's a great feeling when you walk past the aviaries that house your breeding pairs, and birds that are ten or fifteen years old call out to you and say "Hello, Ark Wark." They have not forgotten after all those years.

Communicating with your birds on a regular basis goes a long way to creating a friendly daily working routine. And talking to your birds helps you to get to know them and more importantly gets them to know you. Each morning after the chicks have had their first feed, I load the feeding trolley with the buckets of seed and freshly chopped fruits, fresh rain water, and walk down to where the breeding pairs are housed. By the time I reach the first aviary every adult pair knows I'm coming, although only one or two pairs can see me the word goes out from aviary to aviary. Sometimes I am greeted with "Ark Wark" or "Hello Darling" as I unlock the door to remove the food dishes. It's during this time spent at each aviary that you get to know each pair of birds and over the weeks and months you soon get to feel if anything is wrong with them.

The time you spend with your birds gets you in tune with them. I remember one particular time when I had a group of buyers from Queensland; we had not ventured down to the aviaries and were looking at some of the young Eclectus parrot chicks I had just weaned. Suddenly I heard a sound and without thinking I said there is a black snake down at the birds. My visitors asked me how you knew that there is a snake down there. I said my birds let me know, and sure enough there was a six foot black snake outside one of the aviaries. This happened on many occasions and after a while I could tell just by the sounds the birds made if it was a snake, hawk or cat, because there was a different call for each of them.

Spending quality time out around your birds will certainly go a long way to making them better breeders. With them getting used to you helps the new young breeders to relax and settle down. These young breeders listen to the older birds and settle down a lot more quickly in a relaxed and happier environment.

It should not just be a quick run around the aviaries, a quick look at their seed, throw in a few pieces of fruit each morning and the rest left until the weekend when you have more time. Spend the time!

When the Eclectus parrot chicks that I am hand rearing break color they are leg banded and given a house name. If the chick is a male and is from a breeding pair that has not produced chicks before it then gets a name starting with the letter (A) i.e.Adam. If it is a female and comes from a pair that has bred once before I would call it "Betty." This helps me during the day when I am feeding the breeding pairs to remember which chicks are from which pairs. It's also very helpful when perspective buyers come to remember which particular chick belongs to which aviary.

Most fledglings are sold when you can show prospective buyers the adult parents. Once they see that these youngsters will soon develop into these beautiful looking parrots, these birds almost sell themselves.

I prefer to hand feed my birds with a spoon. Others think this method is somewhat "old hat" and prefer to use specially designed feeding syringes or crop needles. The main thing that worries me with using syringes and crop needles is controlling what the temperature is of the food you are feeding, also the mixture has to be of a thin consistency for it to pass through the feeding tubes.

By using a tea spoon with bent up sides it is more natural for the chick. It's similar to the parents' beak motion when she is feeding her chicks. There is nothing foreign about it and there is no invasion of the chick's throat. It may take a little longer but there is a lot less chance of anything going wrong. The feeding mixture can be kept at the proper feeding temperature and each spoonful can be checked and tested before being fed to the chick. And once chicks are older than ten days of age the feeding mixture is a lot thicker and contains small pieces of fruit and vegetables.

5.5 Fledglings, When to remove them

When Eclectus parrot chicks are around ten weeks old you will find they will start to climb out of the brooder and sit on the edge of the box. Some will even fly to where you are preparing their mixture; this is the time to begin to transfer them to the holding cage.

I have at least two holding cages in my nursery. These are 4ft.x2ft.square, (1.2m x 610mm square). With a perch at each end, anything larger would cause damage to any of the chicks placed inside them if they decided to fly and then miss the perch at the other end. The idea of a smaller cage is just to get them used to perching and climbing around the wire and down to the food dishes to encourage them to start to feed themselves.

When fledglings are removed from the brooder for their first feed of the morning, they are fed and then placed into the holding cage for a couple of hours. Only the chicks that are ten weeks of age or chicks that have started to climb out of the brooder are placed into this cage.

If younger chicks are moved in you will find that they anchor themselves to the perch and are petrified. They just squat and soon fall off onto the wire floor. These birds should be placed back into the brooder and then wait until they show signs of wanting to leave the brooder. After a couple of hours these fledglings should be checked and if they look tired and are just sitting there half asleep then pop them back into the brooder. You will notice right away that they will be happy to be back with the others and go straight into a corner and rest.

I start off by only putting each fledgling in the holding cage once or if it's a nice warm day twice per day, until they are used to sitting on a perch without falling off. Once they have mastered this and look forward to getting into this cage each day, I extend their time in there; this is usually about the second week. Eclectus parrots usually fledge the nest at around twelve weeks of age, although not all the sub species are the same, i.e. the Solomon Island Eclectus leaves the nest at around ten weeks, so the fledging times will depend on what sub species you are breeding. My data relates to the Australian Eclectus, *Eclectus roratus macgillivrayi.* After the end of their second week in the holding cage it's time to leave them out overnight, not outdoors but still in the bird room. Their first night they should be checked a few times and the last time before you go to bed. If they are sitting okay then they will be all right.

I like to leave them a further two weeks before they are then moved outdoors to a larger flight aviary. During these two weeks I observe them and decide which ones I would like to keep as future breeders, and the ones that I would sell. During the time you have been hand feeding these birds you will already have some idea of which ones have something slightly different about them. The size of the head is larger, the overall appearance of the bird is appealing to the eye, the bird is bright and alert, and will be the more active, even more aggressive than some of the others. These are some of the traits I look for when deciding if a particular bird should be kept for future breeding.

As breeders we would love to keep them all, but of course we cannot do this, and the majority of them will be sold as pets or traded to other breeders. In regard to the Australian Eclectus *Eclectus roratus macgillivrayi*, because of their very low numbers in aviculture none of the birds have been sold as pets. And furthermore only unrelated pairs were sold or traded to other Eclectus breeders.

When moving young fledglings outdoors for the first time I try to house them as a group. This group would consist of between four and eight birds of mixed sexes. These birds are kept in age groups, i.e. three months, four months, five months etc. Birds that are six months or younger are housed in large portable suspended aviaries. These aviaries are 12ft.x3ft square (3.6m x 914mm square), this is to help them adjust to a larger aviary and to assimilate with each other. The smaller size aviary is very useful for the first week or so in case you have to remove any of them that have not adjusted to being outdoors or mixing with others. These birds are taken back indoors and given a day or two, then try again to reintroduce them to the group.

Because by this stage all fledglings would have been leg banded so clutches of chicks i.e. brother and sister or two males or two females it doesn't matter they can be kept together. After a month or so they are then transferred to a large flight aviary. This aviary may contain other Eclectus parrot sub species of varying ages, and of both sexes, but all under one year of age. The larger this aviary is, the better it will be for the young fledglings.

While working at the zoo in Broome, and having the luxury of many large flight aviaries to choose from, the young Eclectus parrot fledglings were released into an aviary measuring 25ft.long by 12ft. wide and 8ft high (7.6m.long by 3.6m. wide and 2.4m. high). These aviaries were mostly open with a shelter at one end. There were only three perches, one at the rear under the shelter, one about six feet in front of that one, but still under the shelter and the other at the far end of the open flight. Placing the perches this distance apart encouraged the birds to fly and thus gained exercise and proper wing development.

The feeding tray was also on a stand about two feet off the ground. The birds had to fly and land on the small perch that was attached to this feeding tray. The newly released fledglings would soon learn from the older birds how to fly and land safely on either the feeding tray or the other perches within the aviary.

No nest logs or nest boxes are placed in aviaries housing fledglings. Nest boxes are not provided until birds have reached three years of age.

These large flight aviaries were all fitted with an overhead sprinkler system; these young Eclectus parrot fledglings, as we found out, enjoyed this. The older birds would fly up first and hang upside down from the wire roof of the aviary. The younger ones soon followed them, and due to Broome's hot dry climate this was enjoyed twice a day. Weather permitting Eclectus parrots should be encouraged to bathe at least once a day. It gets them actively involved and further helps to socialize with each other.

During their first twelve months in this aviary each bird is checked and assessed for possible future breeding programs. Any bird that is not required for these programs is moved to another aviary and is sold or traded to other breeders. After the first year the birds that have been retained for future breeding are separated from their siblings and housed in another large flight aviary with other unrelated birds. These birds will be of the same sub species and where possible equal number of males and females. Sometimes as we breeders know too well you can get a run of more males to females in any given year, although it normally balances out within a year or so.

Over the next twelve months these future breeders are watched for signs of pairing up and bonding within the aviary. At two years of age most males are slow to show any signs of wanting to feed or even be close to any of the females. On the other hand females can get to a stage where they endeavor to seek attention from the males. Once a pair of bird's starts showing signs of bonding, their genetic records are checked to make sure that these birds are a suitable match for each other.

It's important when pairing up young future breeders to record their leg band numbers as well as keeping a record of each of their parents' identification numbers. This will ensure that these new birds are not related to each other.

I keep their records on my computer and when any bird is sold or traded a specimen report sheet is printed out which details that particular bird's recorded history such as date of birth, computer identification number, leg band number, parents' identification numbers and aviary number. This specimen report is then sent to the new owners of the bird.

When these young birds are three years old, nest boxes are provided at the start of the breeding season. It's important to have more nesting boxes than there are breeding pairs, i.e. if there are four pairs in the aviary then I install six nest boxes. This will help deter any squabbling over nesting sites. The purpose of these nest boxes is not necessarily to get them to breed, but more importantly to encourage them to explore the possibility of breeding. One thing I learnt from observing them in the wilds of Cape York was that young birds spent a lot of time investigating nesting hollows. Young pairs would spend days at a particular nesting site, and then the next day we would sit all day and not see them. This would go on for days. Young inexperienced pairs would spend months investigating possible nesting sites before they decide to breed. This is all part of the courtship and pair bonding that takes many months or even years to perfect.

When asked, "At what age do they start to breed", most breeders of Eclectus parrots will say "at three years" and this is partly true. Eclectus parrots will start to breed at this age, and some will even produce clutches of healthy chicks. But the majority of them will lay, and lay many clutches of infertile eggs; this can go on for month's even years. Some breeders get so frustrated with their birds they break up the pairs and re-pair them or even sell them to other breeders, then to receive a phone call a few months later from their new owner saying that they have two healthy chicks in the nest. Patience is required in getting these beautiful parrots to breed.

Flying young three-year-old Eclectus parrots in a large flight aviary as a group will go a hell of a long way to overcoming the possibility of having endless nests of infertile eggs. Having four or six unrelated pairs in the one aviary, plus the required number of nesting boxes, will stimulate the females to start scratching up the nesting material in these nest boxes. This in turn will get the males interested in sparring for a mate, by flying and landing on top of the nest box containing the female. She will climb up the ladder poke her head out, and if it's not the male she wants she will chase him off. This will go on until she bonds and then when you see the male feeding the female, it's time to move that pair to a separate breeding aviary of their own. I usually remove the nest she was scratching in as well, in no time she is back working the nest box. At Broome we found that by far this was the best way to pair up future breeding pairs. And if you take the time to observe your birds as we did you will find that this is the best way to pair up unrelated birds and turn them into good fertile producing pairs.

If you have the aviary space then not all the new pairs of Eclectus parrots have to be housed in single breeding flights. Eclectus parrots do very well in with other Eclectus parrots, providing the aviary is large enough, and there are extra nesting sites.

In Broome we tried two pairs of Australian Eclectus parrots in a large planted aviary, this aviary was 120ft.long by 25ft.wide and 15ft.high (36m.long by7.6m.wide and 4.5m.high). This aviary also had a small waterfall and stream running the full length of the aviary. Four nest boxes were provided, two at each end. These pairs bred very well, and

it's worth noting that at all times they nested next to each other—
when one pair changed ends so did the other pair.

We also experimented with eight pairs of New Guinea Eclectus parrots
Eclectus roratus polychloros in one of our largest aviaries. The only
difference between these and the two pairs of Australian Eclectus
parrot was these eight pairs were all mature, bonded and in most cases
breeding pairs. This aviary was about the size of two tennis courts and
was 45ft.high (13.6m.high). It contained fully grown Pandanus palm
Pandanus spiralis trees as well as many other rainforest species. The
eight pairs were released under a soft release program (one pair
released every other day) and after some early squabbling all settled in
fine. Twelve nesting sites were provided. These were all on telescopic
metal pipe stands, which were extended to various heights among the
pandanus palms.

Within a matter of weeks we had a number of pairs nesting. Some
pairs swapped mates but all in all this colony breeding system worked
very well. So breeding Eclectus parrots together in a communal aviary
should be tried if you have the aviary space and the required number
of pairs to make it work, but please do not mix sub species.

5.6 Sale, Permits, Boxing and Shipping

When breeding Eclectus parrots for sale either as pets or as future
young breeding pairs, it is important to have them arrive at their new
owners unstressed and in good condition. Most sales are to customers
that live some distance away, either in another city, town or interstate.
These customers rely on your honesty and reputation to receive their
birds quickly and without mishap.

Most orders and sales are received by phone, either by reading your
advertisement in the local bird magazine or by word of mouth; the
latter is the preferred way to establish your bird breeding reputation.
Once you are well known for breeding Eclectus parrots, which are of

good quality, and of a pure sub species, you will soon develop that reputation.

When a sale is received over the phone the buyer is purchasing these birds sight unseen, he will be relying on your judgement and assessment of them. He will also be relying on your capacity to catch them, box them and arrange the shipping details for them, and then deliver them to the airport. Until these birds are consigned and received at the freight depot they are your responsibility.

Do you ask for a deposit? This is something breeders have to decide for themselves. If they are a first time customer and they order a pair of birds that are still in the process of being hand reared then I usually ask for a 1/3 deposit and the balance paid, including shipping cost, before they are dispatched. If the purchasers are regular customers and are well known to me, then I waive the deposit, but on no account do I ship birds without full payment, especially to dealers or pet storeowners.

Shipping bird's interstate usually requires permits to do so. Most states here in Australia require an export permit if the birds are native birds. Some states require import permits for all birds entering that state; each exotic bird is assessed for its pest potential and in some cases is banned from entering that state. So it pays to be up to date on the interstate laws pertaining to live import/export of birds. Here in this country the importer (purchaser) has to obtain his import permit first. This can take as little time as it takes to fax it to you. In some states you have to apply in writing before a permit is issued, and this can take up to two weeks. So it pays to plan ahead. Once you have a copy of the purchaser's import permit then you can apply for your export permit.

Once the permits are in place it's then time to organize a suitable flight that is (1) suitable for the person receiving your birds, arriving in daylight so the birds do not have to spend the night in the shipping box. (2) Try and organize a direct flight (most birds are lost or sent to the wrong destination due to being transferred from one flight to another). (3) Allow enough time to catch the birds and settle them down before taking them to the airport. And (4) most airlines insist on having freight at the freight depot one hour before the scheduled flight is due to leave, so it will pay to get to know the manager personally so you can have an arrangement by where you can deliver them closer to the flight time.

If for some reason birds have to overnight during their flight to their destination, I ask the shipping agent, when I book the birds on, to fax their counterpart at the stopover point, to alert them to the shipment of live birds. When I return home I also follow up with a fax to the same agent detailing whom they are going to and their flight details for the next day. If there are alterations to the flight times that I have given the purchasers, I phone them and notify them of the changes. I also ask all my customers to phone me once their new birds are released into their new home to see if they are happy with them and are satisfied with the boxing and shipping arrangements.

After a few weeks it's worth making a follow up phone call to see how the birds have settled in, and more importantly if the new owners are satisfied with their pair of Eclectus parrots. Also at this time ongoing advice is offered if they are ever in need of it. You would be surprised how much new owners respect this kind of offer, and furthermore an offer such as this could lead to the possibility of further sales to their friends.

Some of my customers ask if I guarantee my birds! This in itself is a tricky situation, as we all know the "bird game" has a lot of (for want of a better word) "shady characters" among us. This reminds me of story that I believe to this day to be true, and it goes like this ... A breeder in one of our southern states ordered a shipment of birds from a "well-known breeder." These birds were expensive and at that time not many were available. He paid the money over and waited for his shipment to arrive. The shipment arrived on time and when he got them home he found a couple of birds dead in the box. He quickly phoned the breeder that sent him the birds to ask if he would send him a couple more to make up for the two dead ones, or would he refund him the difference. His answer was "once the birds left the airport they become your responsibility." What the purchaser did not tell the sender was one of the birds was still frozen when he first opened the shipping box. What this guy was doing was any time a bird died in his aviaries, he would put it in his freezer and every now and then he would put one or two of them in shipments going interstate, then claiming it must have died in transit and it was then the problem of the receiver of the birds.

Having the purchaser of the birds phone you once they have released their birds into the aviary, and then following that up with a call two weeks later to see if they are happy with the birds, will help to overcome any of these problems. Breeders that I know and my regular customers I guarantee the birds for 48 hours after they receive them. If for any reason they are unhappy with them I ask that they let me know within that time. We discuss the matter and try and resolve it. In most cases these people are first time Eclectus parrot owners and may have only seen them in books or a matured pair at another breeder's aviaries. As breeders of these birds we are used to these young birds looking drab when they are only six months old, but to these first time Eclectus parrot owners they expect them to look like the ones they had seen themselves.

Once everything is explained to them most will accept them. I tell them to call me in twelve months and let me know what they think of them then. Most of them never do, except to order another pair.

When an order is received and the necessary permits have been obtained its then time to prepare the shipping box. There is a lot of conjecture over what constitutes the perfect shipping box— some airlines and wildlife authorities have a set of guidelines that you can adopt, so check with these departments to see if they have any special requirements.

When deciding on the design of the shipping box very few people consider the bird's point of view— they just want a box that is small and is light in weight, because these are the points that determine the cost of freighting these birds to their customers. But the customers are charged for this boxing and freight costs so why not spend a little extra time and effort in designing a box that is suitable for the birds. Most shipping boxes have open wire fronts; to me this is very stressing for the birds, every time handlers during transport pick up the birds they flap their wings and rush to the rear of the box. This style of box is completely open to the elements. Shipping boxes are often left out on the tarmac between flights, and this could be freezing cold or blistering hot depending on where they are being shipped.

Because shipping boxes are usually only used the once I decided to use a cardboard apple carton. These are sturdy and easy to obtain from local fruit merchants who are only too glad to get rid of them. The lid of the carton which has all the advertising on it is undone and reversed (turned inside out) so that the advertising is not seen. This is then glued back together, this leaves me with a clean fresh looking plain cardboard box. I then make up a 19 inch long by 11inch square (482mm. long by 279mm.square) wire mesh cage that fits snugly inside the apple carton. This cage is made out of off cuts of inch by inch (25mm.by 25mm.) bird wire, the same that is used on my breeding aviaries. The door is cut into the top of this cage, and is large enough that I can get both my hands inside. Be sure to file the ends of the wire where the door has been cut out of; also file the sides of the door to remove any sharp points. The door also overlaps the hole so the birds cannot pull it in. The reason for the door at the top of the cage is the lid of the carton then fits over the cage that has been fitted into the bottom section of the carton. And after the birds have been placed inside, and the top of the carton placed back over it, it is then taped down. When the birds arrive at their destination it's then just a simple matter to cut the tape, lift the lid and inspect the birds. I do not provide a perch when shipping Eclectus parrots; instead I cover the bottom of the box and the wire mesh floor with a layer of clean nesting material, or dry wood mulch. This is soft on the birds' feet and absorbs their droppings. I have found that shipping Eclectus parrots this way is far less stressful on the birds as the inside of this enclosed box is similar to the inside of a nest box.

If the young pair of birds that are being shipped have been housed together and are compatible with each other, then they are shipped together. If the birds have not been housed together, I then divide the shipping box, and provide two doors, to insure that there is no fighting between them.

The holes provided in the carton for easy handling will be sufficient for the amount of fresh air the birds will require during transit. If it is hot weather at the time of shipping then a series of small holes are punched into each side using a pencil or screwdriver, be sure to do this before the birds are placed inside.

When it's time to catch the birds and place them in the shipping box, make sure that everything is ready because this needs to be carried out quickly and calmly. Have enough food such as apple cut into quarters, a piece of orange, banana, and half a corncob, plus greens such as lettuce, silver beet, and a small amount of budgie mix seed. No water is provided and providing they have plenty of juicy type of fruits they will not require it. In fact few birds eat or drink much at all during shipping, but it will make you feel a lot better if you provide them with plenty of fruit. Also when the purchasers receive them they will see that they at least had plenty to eat and will not have to worry about them being hungry if they have a long drive home.

I usually catch the birds about half an hour before I'm due to leave for the airport. This allows me enough time to have them boxed, the wire door wired shut and the lid of the carton placed over them, I let them sit for a few minutes before I tape it up, just to make sure everything is okay. If there is no squabbling then it's time to tape them up and stick on the necessary labels.

Proper labels are very important for the shipping of live birds, they need to be the stick on type, and these are available from the airline shipping agents. It's also important to remember that these birds are in a box and a box to the busy freight handlers is just another piece of freight. These freight handlers are only interested in the consignment note that details the flight it is to go on. They don't have the time to read labels that are just written on the box with a black felt pen. By using the proper stick on type of labels the freight handlers will know at a glance that the box contains live birds, because it will have a live animal sticker attached to the top of the box. They are trained to recognize these labels.

On each shipping box I attach the following labels, (1) the main address label, this details the names and address and phone number of the sender, the name and address and phone number of the receiver. **Live Animal-With Care** typed in large bold lettering plus "Please keep out of direct sunlight." It also has a section that reads "On arrival please contact" in which is written the contact phone number of who the birds are going to. (2) The consignment note (supplied by the airline freight depot). Be sure that this is filled in and is readable. This is attached to the bottom right hand side of the lid. The con note as it is known is the label that the freight handlers take notice of. It contains all the relevant flight details as well as the names and addresses of both the sender and receiver. The sender retains a copy of this consignment note in case the box of birds ends up on another flight or gets lost. This consignment note is the only way they will be able to track the box down and return it to its destination.

(3) The live animal sticker is the next important sticker to be fixed onto the box; I stick on five of these per box, one on the lid next to the main address label and then one per side of the box. The live animal stickers may vary from state to state or from country to country but most display four animal images and these are 1) Dog, 2) Bird, 3) Fish, 4) Tortoise. Circle the bird image with a red felt pen to indicate that the box contains live birds.

(4) The next sticker is the "This side up" sticker. I fix four of these stickers on per box, and I place them right next to the live bird stickers, one on each side. These are the sticker most people forget to attach to their shipping boxes, and there is nothing worse when you see your birds being unloaded from the aircraft to see them placed upside down on the freight trolley.

(5) The airport collect sticker. This sticker indicates that the birds are to be collected personally by the receiver at the airport freight office. The freight handlers will know by this sticker that the birds have to be held until collected. If the box is not clearly labeled with this sticker for collection at the airport then it could end up at another freight depot in the city. I place two of these stickers on the lid of the box one on the right-hand side and the other on the left-hand side.

(6) The two remaining stickers are the destination sticker supplied by the airline and the clear plastic wallet sticker that you enclose your import/export permits in. The destination sticker is filled out by the freight handler and will show where the freight was shipped from, the date, the con note number, the number of boxes and the weight of the consignment. The clear plastic wallet is attached to the bottom left hand corner of the lid of the box and any permits that are to accompany the shipment are placed inside this wallet. This allows for easy inspection by wildlife officers and in some cases quarantine officers at various interstate airports.

I also take the precaution of writing my name address and contact number as well as the receiver's contact details with a black felt pen somewhere on the box, just in case some of the stickers are removed.

Whichever style of shipping box you decide to use at least be sure that due consideration is given to the birds' needs during this procedure. Boxing and shipping can be stressful on the birds and a little extra effort can go a long way in making the shipping process a little less stressful for you and the birds.

Chapter 6
Keeping Eclectus Parrots Healthy

Keeping your Eclectus parrots healthy and in excellent feather condition is the most important way to insure they become good breeders and long time producing pairs. If a first time owner of Eclectus parrots then get to know other breeders in your area, ask their advice on the best way to care for them, read as much material as you can lay your hands on about these fascinating birds. And more importantly ask them to recommend the best local avian veterinarian.

Over the past ten years or so there has been a growing emergence of avian veterinarians, due mainly to the surgical sexing boom. This has been great for aviculture; now we have experienced veterinarians specializing in all the aspects of aviculture. Many of these avian veterinarians are breeders as well; they are eagerly accepted into our local bird clubs and societies, often speaking and answering questions at club meetings and conventions.

Getting to know your local avian veterinarian, on a first name basis will be even better, it will allow you to phone him whenever you have a problem. In the past us breeders had to fend for ourselves; veterinarians knew little or nothing about birds and many birds were lost due to not receiving the proper care and treatment. Thankfully that has all changed now due to these dedicated avian veterinarians.

As breeders of Eclectus parrots "preventive medicine" is the best medicine, by providing our birds with open flight aviaries with plenty of room to fly and to exercise their wings, and providing a balanced fruit and vegetable, minimal seed and pellet diet. Provide fresh branches at least twice a week, some containing blossoms and buds and others containing seeds. Resist the temptation of giving them something extra such as pasta, pizza, and table scraps. Avoid feeding them items such as nuts that contain fatty oils, one pecan nut twice a week per bird is enough for these birds.

I would avoid feeding chicken meat or bones to Eclectus parrots. It would be far better to add a few mealworms or termites to their diet than feed them oily meat such as chicken meat. Let's not forget that these parrots are arboreal parrots and their natural diet is what they can find in the rainforest canopy. Their diet in the wild consists of native fruits, seeds, leaf buds and blossoms that contain nectar. One of the most popular fruits that are a favorite of Eclectus parrots are native figs, notably the cluster fig *Ficus racemosa*. These bright red and orange figs grow on the trunk and upper branches of the tree and are easily foraged by feeding Eclectus parrots. These ripe figs when opened contain larvae of the fig wasps *(Agaonidae)*. Way back in 1972, I was trying to breed Red-browed Fig parrots *Cyclopsitta diophthalma macleayana* for the first time in captivity. And on studying these tiny birds in the wild I discovered that they were not eating the fruit pulp of these figs but eating the wasp larvae that was a live parasite inside.

Do Eclectus parrots do the same? I am sure they do, but further study of their feeding habits in the wild would have to be carried out to confirm this. It is also quite probable that Eclectus parrots feed on termites found under bark and inside nesting hollows. So keeping our birds healthy by trying to feed them a diet that is as close to their natural diet as possible would be a far better way to maintain these birds in perfect breeding condition than by giving them junk food!

As you know by now I am a breeder and not an avian veterinarian, so as breeders what basics do we need to know before calling in the avian veterinarian? We have already covered two of the main points and these are (1) Housing, and (2) Diet. Some other basics points are routine husbandry, how to recognize a sick bird, what to do with a sick bird and basic treatment.

Routine husbandry are the daily tasks that we carry out each day, like food preparation, making sure that the food is fresh clean and all the food containers have been washed and are ready for use. Never place fresh food on top of old food! Remove the leftovers of food from the day before and replace the food bowls with clean ones. Water bowls should be scrubbed and filled with fresh clean water. Clean or replace any dirty or broken perches (dirty perches are the main source of bacteria). Birds clean their beaks by rubbing them up and down the edges of their perch. Rake the floor of the open flight and remove the bird's droppings from the concrete floor of the shelter, then hose it down.

I prefer to use glazed earthenware bowls for both food and water. These are easy to clean and are heavy enough that the birds do not turn them over and they come in various sizes and depth. My next choice would be stainless steel containers. Plastic containers should be avoided.

How do we recognize a sick bird? What do we look for? These are questions I am often asked by new owners of Eclectus parrots. In time as breeders we develop a sixth sense about our birds and can tell the moment we look at them that something is wrong. I start each morning before I prepare the morning feed out by walking around all the aviaries. I walk slowly talking to each pair, if I get a feeling that something is just not right with a particular bird, then the first thing that I do is inspect its droppings. This will be the first place you would notice if something was wrong. By looking at the colour and texture of the bird's droppings will indicate if this bird should be removed and isolated for treatment. Normal droppings are dark green with a fair amount of white mixed with it. If the dropping is pale green or yellowish or even brown in colour then this indicates to me that there is a problem.

Depending on the time of year e.g. winter, then the bird is removed into a holding cage inside the bird room. If it's during the summer months then I may leave it in its aviary, but monitor it closely. If no improvement is noticed by late afternoon then it's removed inside. Once inside the bird is monitored for 24 hours to see if it's feeding; after 24 hours if the bird looks no better then the avian veterinarian is contacted for advice on the proper course of treatment. The other thing I look for when doing my morning inspection of the birds, as well as looking at bird's droppings. Is look for any bird sitting fluffed up, that is a bird that sits with either its head bent back and under its wing or sits with its eyes closed and its feathers fluffed up? This is a sure sign that something is amiss. This bird will also have the pale droppings and should be removed and isolated. The avian veterinarian should be contacted immediately for advice and treatment.

When any sick bird is isolated precautions should be taken to make sure that whatever this bird has is contained. After examination by the avian veterinarian and a course of treatment is prescribed all feeding bowls and perches inside the holding cage should be washed daily and disinfected and not used in any other cage or aviary until the sick bird has completely recovered. Even then these bowls and perches are again washed and disinfected and left outside in the sun for a couple of days. I put white butcher's paper in the metal tray under the perches to monitor the bird's droppings while the sick bird's in the holding cage. The same way we determined that this bird was sick will be the same way we determine if the bird is well again. By looking at its droppings, when its droppings return to normal then in a few days this bird will be fit enough to return it to its original aviary. Be sure to finish the course of treatment prescribed by your avian veterinarian before returning any sick bird back to its aviary.

Basic treatment! As breeders we should be able to provide at least some sort of basic treatment for the birds in our care. To this end I keep four types of medication on hand in my bird room. **1.** Friar's balsam, a Benzoin compound Tincture for the treatment of cuts and bleeding toes (also ideal for the many bites that you receive to your hands from handling Eclectus parrots). **2.** Nilstat® a Nystatin based medication for the treatment of Candidiasis, a fungal infection found inside the mouth and inside the bird's crop. Candidiasis found in Eclectus parrots is usually due to bad or below standard of husbandry and can also be linked to the lack of the nutritional requirements in the way of fresh fruit and vegetables that is lacking in their daily diet. Birds that have this infection should be isolated from all other birds as Candidiasis is highly contagious and can be transmitted to us humans if we don't wash our hands carefully after treating or feeding these sick birds.

Consult your avian veterinarian for advice if Candidiasis is suspected, he will advise on the dose rate and the duration of the treatment.

3. Worming solution. If Eclectus parrots are housed in open flighted aviaries and are able to venture onto the ground, then they will require worming twice a year. I worm my birds at the start of spring and again at the end of autumn. I use Avitrolplus wormer syrup that is administered by adding it to the drinking water, it can also be given direct to the beak. I prefer to add it to their drinking water. I do this by leaving their water bowls empty for most of the day. Then adding the medicated solution to their water at about 3pm in the afternoon, you will find that most of the birds will come down to drink straight away. This worming solution is left for 24 hours and then the whole process is repeated 14 days later.

If Eclectus parrots are housed in suspended aviaries and no contact is made with the ground then worming treatment is advisable only once a year at the beginning of spring. It's worth noting here that if the wire mesh on your aviaries permits the entry of wild native birds into the aviary then worming twice a year would be recommended. Worms are transmitted through the droppings of other birds.

4. When you have become personally acquainted with your local avian veterinarian and the next time he pays you a visit, get him to show you how to administer antibiotic medication by injection. Everyone hates to use these things, but they are essential for the speedy treatment of sick birds. Birds respond quicker to medication when it's injected into the pectoral muscle (breast muscle) of the sick bird. Its affect is immediate! After you have done it a few times it becomes second nature, and by administering it this way the bird cannot regurgitate it in the way it does if given by mouth.

The injectable antibiotic that I use is called "Linco-Spectin"® made by Upjohn Pty. Ltd. of Sydney and is available through your avian veterinarian. If you are not experienced in giving injections then consult with your avian veterinarian and have him do it for you. This injectable antibiotic that I use has to be given twice a day so having the veterinarian call twice a day for the course of the treatment can become costly, but you have to weigh up what's more important, the cost, or the sick bird's health. When you have to inject a sick Eclectus parrot twice a day be sure to alternate each injection site. First injection into the right hand side of the sternal keel into the breast muscle, and the next to the left-hand side. This will help to alleviate any bruising to the muscle.

Antibiotics are improving every day so ask your avian veterinarian regularly for an update on any improvements to this medication.

In all my years of keeping and breeding Eclectus parrots there has been one problem that keeps popping up every now and then: "feather plucking." Is it a disease? Is it physiological or a psychological problem?

There is nothing worse than coming out one morning, walking around your birds doing the usual morning inspection, then notice one of your best birds that you paid a lot of money for, plucking itself. Like most breeders I have tried everything to overcome this problem and to date I do not have any answers.

Even some of the best avian veterinarians cannot come up with the proper answer to the feather plucking problem. What I do know about this problem is that it seems to be more prevalent in certain sub species than others. For example I don't recall ever having a case of feather plucking with any of our New Guinea Eclectus parrots *Eclectus roratus polychloros,* yet they were housed and fed the same. Feather plucking seems to affect the Vosmaeri Eclectus parrot, *Eclectus roratus vosmaeri* the most, followed by the Australian Eclectus, *Eclectus roratus macgillivrayi* and the Grand Eclectus parrot, *Eclectus roratus roratus,* that is at least here in Australia.

My personal feelings about this problem are that a lot of it is to do with stress. Stress comes in many forms; it can be as simple as how you enter their aviary, do you announce that you are entering? Do you sometimes wear a hat and other times you don't? Even wearing different coloured clothing has an effect on these birds. An example of this relates back to when I was curator of birds at the zoo in Broome. In the early days our bird keepers, and mammal keepers for that matter, were permitted to wear street clothes while feeding out in their sections. Some keepers would wear hats or caps of various colors, as well as a variety of colored clothing. What we observed was the birds and even some of the mammals stressed out when certain colors were worn. After discussions with the owner of the zoo, Lord McAlpine, we decided to issue uniforms to all our keeping staff.

We consulted with other zoos and bird parks here in Australia and overseas for their advice on the preferred color for these uniforms. After taking into account Broome's location and climate we decided to provide polo shirts and "T" shirts in a plain gray/green color and asked our keepers to wear similar colored shorts and hats. This had an immediate affect on the birds and animals and the stress level was dramatically reduced.

Feather plucking is less likely to occur if Eclectus parrots are housed in spacious open flight aviaries, or housed as a group. Eclectus parrots do not like being confined in small enclosures, as they easily become bored with their surroundings. Boredom leads to stress and this leads them to begin plucking themselves. Pet Eclectus parrots that are kept in small display cages have their owners to keep them occupied; they also spend long periods outside their cage interacting with people, therefore have a much less of a chance of becoming bored and start being destructive to their feathers.

Physiological or psychological? I personally think it can be both! For example we had a breeding pair of Australian Eclectus parrots, *Eclectus roratus macgillivrayi* that was one of our regular producing pairs. The male, a huge bird in size, was starting to pluck itself at the nape of its neck, between both wings. This area was about the size of a matchbox. I never noticed it actually pulling the feathers out while I was cleaning or feeding them of a morning so I decided to monitor them at certain times during the day. What I noticed was that just after they were fed each morning, and after the female had been down to eat, and after she had returned to the nest box, he would come down to the seed dish and start placing whole sunflower seeds on this bare patch at the back of his neck. He would place about five or six seeds there and for a moment or two, do nothing, just sit there, then he would crack and eat the sunflower seeds and returned to the seed dish for more. This would go on until he had satisfied his hunger, things then returned to normal.

Was this a game to amuse himself, while the female incubated her eggs? I feel that this was part of the problem. This pair was housed in a portable suspended aviary 12ft. X 3ft. Square (3.6m. X 914mm. Square) with the nest box fitted on the outside of the aviary, this was probably two small an aviary for this the largest sub species of Eclectus parrots.

My observations of this sub species in the wilds of Cape York demonstrated to me that these Eclectus parrots loved flying and were very active birds. I rarely, if ever, saw them just sitting around doing nothing. If they weren't feeding or chasing females, they were in a group of males including young birds from the previous breeding season playing with each other. They were constantly on the move flying around as a group or accompanying females checking out nesting hollows. They were very fit and active birds.

I think that in captivity we tend to house them in aviaries that are far too small, aviaries that lack the flight space that is required for these birds. I would strongly suggest that we review how we are housing them at present, and if we are serious about breeding them properly, then make the necessary changes.

In all the years of watching Eclectus parrots in the wild I cannot recall ever seeing a feather plucked bird, so one would have to assume that it's a problem related to captivity. So constructing better aviaries with longer flights and providing a more natural environment in the way of native plants and shrubs will go a long way in preventing feather plucking in these birds. There are three main factors that could cause Eclectus parrots to feather pluck, these are **1.** Housing, **2.** Diet, and **3.** Stress. Unsuitable housing plus an inadequate diet leads to stress and stress leads to feather plucking.

Two of these points above are covered in previous chapters but it may be prudent to raise them again here. The housing of Eclectus parrots as pairs in suitable size aviaries, the minimum size required for each pair should be 24ft. long by 6ft.wide by 8ft. high, (7.3m.long by 1.8m. wide by 2.4m high) with at least two thirds being open flight area (open to the elements such as rain and sunshine). If intending to house Eclectus parrots as groups of say five pairs then an aviary as large as possible i.e. 40ft. long by 12ft. wide by 8ft. high (12.1m. long by 3.6m. wide by 2.4m. high) would be something in the order suitable for that number of birds. Both of these aviaries should also be planted with suitable plants and shrubs.

The diet for these breeding pairs should be as close to a natural diet as possible, by providing fresh fruits and vegetables daily and little or no seed. If seed has to be fed then only budgie breeder's mix and sunflower seed should be added twice a week as a treat and in very small quantities. It would be far better to provide freshly cut eucalyptus branches that contain bush nuts and blossoms, than feed them seed and foods that are not natural for them.

Chapter 7
Companion Eclectus in the United States

By Laurella Desborough

During the seventies and eighties, Eclectus parrots as pets were relatively uncommon in the United States. In fact, they were seldom encountered in pet stores or with bird breeders. When breeders did work with Eclectus parrots, they generally only had one or maybe two pair in their breeding collection.

Eclectus parrots were somewhat expensive and hard to find, with individual birds being priced at US$1500 each and proven pairs at US$3500 to US$4500 per pair. Additionally, since these birds were not common, the various sub species were not readily recognized. Of the four sub species available in the U.S. at the time, The Grand Eclectus *Eclectus roratus roratus,* the Redsided or New Guinea Eclectus *Eclectus roratus polychloros,* the Vosmaeri Eclectus *Eclectus roratus vosmaeri,* and the Solomon Island Eclectus *Eclectus roratus solomonensis.* The Solomon Island Eclectus was the rarest and the most expensive.

By the nineties, Eclectus parrots were better known, with a higher profile in the bird magazines such as *Bird Talk* and the American Federation of Aviculture magazine *Watchbird.* In the early nineties as the Wild Bird Conservation Act was under consideration in the U.S. the exporters in the Solomon Islands decided to make Solomon Island Eclectus available for export to the United States. Prior to this time, they had refused to export these birds into the U.S. bird trade. Up until the importation of wild caught birds was closed by the passage of the WBCA into law, hundreds of Solomon Island Eclectus were shipped into the U.S. These birds were made available at relatively low prices, US$1500.a pair, and some bird breeders bought ten to twenty pairs of the Solomons. As of this writing, probably the Solomon Island Eclectus parrot is the most common Eclectus parrot subspecies that remains relatively pure since its small size makes it more easily distinguished from the larger subspecies.

Early breeders of Eclectus provided the information and expertise in their care and handling. Two individuals in the San Francisco Bay area were Marguerite Winn who bred Solomons exclusively and Anna Fredrikson who bred four different sub species of Eclectus parrots. Marguerite had a small collection of Solomons that came from the small shipment imported in the seventies. Both of these ladies were helpful to individuals who wanted to learn how to breed and raise Eclectus parrots. There were no handrearing formulas in those days and they devised formulas that had to be made by combining various ingredients and which provided proper nutrition for Eclectus chicks.

At the present time, Eclectus parrots are still not as widely known in the United States as African grays, Amazons or the large Macaws and Cockatoos, but they are more widely kept as companion birds than at any previous time. Routinely one sees photos of Eclectus parrots in bird magazines advertising and in photos and articles about parrots. This was not the case ten years ago. I speculate that there are at least 5000 companion Eclectus in the U.S. at this time, with the Vosmaeri and the Solomon Island being the most common. Knowledge about the care and handling of Eclectus parrots has become more widespread, but there are still areas of Eclectus management where the lack of information continues to have negative consequences for these birds. Those areas include housing, diet and handling.

Housing Companion Eclectus

Cages. Critical for a happy healthy Eclectus parrot is a cage that is roomy and not constricting. A minimum size recommendation would be a cage that is three foot wide and two feet deep by three foot tall,

(914mm.Wide and 610mm. deep by 914mm. tall). A better size would be three feet by three feet or three feet by four feet, (914mm. By 914mm. or 914mm. By 1.219m.). Eclectus parrots when healthy are very active birds and enjoy swings and springy spiral hanging devices in their cage, as long it does not restrict their movements. Cages with metal bars that are arranged so that the bar spacing is reduced to a point where the bars meet are problems. The birds can get their heads and toes caught in the space reduction area. Cage manufacturers produce cages of various bar spacing and they make recommendations about what spacing is best for each species. Personally, I have not found that bar spacing is a problem for Eclectus. Spacing even up to one and a half inches (38mm) seems to work fine. Of more critical concern is the material from which the cage is made. Stainless steel is highly recommended, although expensive as it is easiest to clean and the most sanitary material. Other types of cage coating need to be reviewed to make sure that the coating does not readily come off when a bird uses its beak on the bars.

Perches. Eclectus parrots do best on perches of softer woods that provide them the opportunity to work their beaks and to keep the beaks groomed by chewing on the softwoods. Hardwoods like eucalyptus and manzanita or other materials such as plastics are not recommended as perches for these birds. In the U.S. softwoods such as fir or cactus skeletons (cholla) are desirable. When Eclectus parrots do not have the opportunity to chew on softwoods, they can develop overgrown beaks. It is important to start youngsters with softwood perches so that they establish this grooming habit early. Young birds that do not learn to chew on softwoods can learn not to chew at all. Those individuals that do not chew on perches or wooden toys are the ones most likely to have overgrown beaks, which require routine trimming by their owner or the veterinarian.

Toys. Eclectus parrots enjoy toys immensely and they are quite excited about any new toys that are introduced into their cage. As much as Eclectus parrots enjoy their toys, they can also become bored with them. For this reason we recommend that the cage toys be rotated on a weekly basis. This also provides the owner with the opportunity to clean the toys of food particles or feces. It is important to purchase only toys in sealed bags when purchasing from pet stores. The sealed bag prevents the toy from being exposed to the dust, dander and viral particles from other birds or animals in the pet store and from the hands of customers looking through the toys. Interesting toys for Eclectus parrots are generally a combination of hard unbreakable colored plastics intermixed with softwoods, sometimes colored, and cut into various shaped with holes in the center. These plastics and wooden shapes are then placed on raw leather cords and hung in the cage along one wall or over a perch area. Eclectus parrots also enjoy toys that contain music that is activated by pushing a button. Special toys for shredding are important and can be made from newspaper or clean cardboard or purchased at the pet store. Some of the small hand toys used for play with small dogs are also ideal for Eclectus parrots, especially when they are young and in the exploratory stage where they want to test everything with their beaks and tongues.

Dangerous Toys. Toys that are dangerous include those with breakable parts, those that can ensnare a toenail or a beak in a narrow space in the toy, or long dangling cords or chains. An Eclectus parrot loves to hang onto hanging toys and will work on the toy to the point that parts can be wrapped around the bird's neck and strangle it. Therefore, with hanging toys, it is recommended that sections of cord or chain be interspersed with sections of straight metal segments which can also hold wooden pieces but the material cannot be wrapped around the bird's neck. Toys with loose cords that can entangle a bird's toenails are also a problem and can result in a broken leg or foot or a chewed toe, as well as a highly stressed bird.

Play Stands. Often cages come with play stands on top, usually consisting of a perch and a couple of feed dishes and perhaps an area where toys can be attached. These cage-top play areas are great for older Eclectus parrots and they do enjoy them a lot. With young

Eclectus parrots that are weaned and learning to live in a new home, these cage-top play areas may be considered by the bird as very desirable. When they are sitting on that high perch atop the cage, they often do not want to step onto your outstretched upreaching hand. Therefore, it is recommended that the owner also have a portable play stand, one that is moveable on rollers and can be relocated as desired, or one that is stationary and can be carried easily from place to place. Play areas should always be provided with food items and with toys. If one uses a separate play stand as well as the cage-top play area for the bird; the bird may enjoy flying back and forth between the two locations. This situation helps the bird identify those two areas as play stations and main sites for landing after flying about the house. Otherwise, a flighted pet bird is likely to discover and claim an area that the owner does not want to be a play area.

Food and Water Bowls. It is recommended that food and water bowls be of a good quality stainless steel as they can be thoroughly disinfected. Some of the Ceramic bowls, although quite attractive, do pose a problem as the birds often chip the glazed surface with their beak during a test of the edge. They may push and pull on the bowl until it drops and breaks unless it is locked into position. It is recommended that each Eclectus cage have three bowls; one for soft foods, one for dry foods and one for water. Some people prefer to use water bottles for their birds, but the birds do have to learn how to use these bottles before the regular water bowls are removed from the cage. Also, water bottles do need to be changed daily just like water bowls. Although the water bottle cannot get major pieces of debris in it, many designs do allow for some back flushing of small particles from the bird's beak and tongue during the drinking process. This, of course, becomes a solution that encourages bacterial growth in the water bottle.

Ceramic Bowls. If Ceramic bowls are used for Eclectus parrots, they should not be of the type that is a low fire Ceramic with bright yellow and red colors, as these Ceramics often use heavy metals in the coloring agents and eventually this can leach into the food or water unless the Ceramic sealing agent is quite secure. When Ceramic bowls become slightly cracked or broken around the edge, they should be replaced as these cracks and breaks become sites that can harbor dangerous gram-negative bacteria.

Bowl Cleaning. It is helpful to have two sets of all bowls so that while one set is in use, the other set can be washed and stored for use the next day. Washing in hot soapy water removes most obvious material, but may not remove all bacterial, viral or fungal agents from the bowls. It is recommended that after the bowls are well rinsed that they be disinfected in a solution of chlorine bleach and water at least once a week. Whenever there are sick birds in the house, the food bowls for the sick bird should be maintained separately and all food and water bowls disinfected daily in order to prevent potential transmission of disease. By the way, placing chlorine bleach in soapy dishwater destroys the disinfecting action of the bleach. Bleach should be prepared in cool water, using one half cup per gallon (4.5 litres) of water to achieve a disinfecting solution. Of course, all disinfected bowls should be well rinsed and drained, then stored in a clean place prior to use.

Diet. If there is one area where many opinions are found, it is in the area of diet. First, we wish to mention a cautionary note regarding the use of vitamin and mineral supplements provided on a daily basis for a companion Eclectus parrot. It is preferred that the owner feed the bird a diet of fresh foods and clean seeds with some pellets rather than to feed only a seed diet and expect Eclectus to be healthy because additional vitamin supplements are provided. Over the last fifteen years a variety of problems have emerged that have been found to have their origin in the use of man made or processed vitamin and mineral supplements that are added to the bird's diet. The use of these supplements has created sufficient problems that avian veterinarian's caution about their use and express their concern about vitamin toxicity. One of the most common problems, toe tapping, is often caused by over supplementation. This muscle spasm in the feet causes the toes to open and close on the perch in a rhythmic manner, producing a clicking sound on the perch, thus the name, toe tapping.

Fresh Vegetables. Greens are perhaps one of the most critical of the fresh foods and one item that is not always provided by the pet owner. In the U.S. such greens as Swiss chard, endive, dandelion, bok choy and spinach are well accepted by Eclectus parrots and will often be the first item selected from the soft food bowl. Broccoli, red and green bell peppers, sliced cucumbers with seeds, slices of lightly baked sweet potatoes or yams, various squashes, whole green beans, chopped celery, corn on the cob, and tomatoes are relished. All vegetables should be well washed and rinsed to remove traces of pesticides and gram negative bacteria from the fields and from the crop pickers and food processors.

Fruits. Eclectus parrots enjoy a variety of fruits but do not seem to like fruits that are over ripe or soft. They readily consume kiwi fruit slices, pomegranate seedlets, papaya including seeds, apple pieces, grapes, pears, various melons with seeds, blueberries, cranberries, cherries, peach slices, and also various exotic fruits such as star fruit. The major concern is to carefully wash and rinse all items presented to the bird. In order to keep their perches cleaner, it is recommended that the seedlets from such fruits as pomegranates be removed from the fruit rather than providing the bird with a large piece of pomegranate. Also, the juice from these seedlets will stain the walls if the cage is positioned too close to the wall. If an individual bird does not seem to touch one fruit or other food item that item should be prepared in different sizes and shapes, from slices to dices, or placed on a skewer and hung in the cage near a perch to tempt the bird to eat it.

Seeds. As with everything, variety is important. One seed item most Eclectus parrots relish is spray millet. They will diligently remove the tiny millet seeds and hull them. The most desirable seed mixes contain many different seeds from small proso millets, to hemp, paddy rice, hard and soft wheat, oat groats, whole corn, and dried red peppers. A few safflower and sunflower seeds, triticale, and dried fruit pieces and vegetable pieces but do not contain added man-made vitamins or minerals.

Sprouted Seeds. It is believed to be quite beneficial to sprout seeds for Eclectus parrots, as the nutrition packaged in a sprouted seed is greater than that in an inert dry seed. Especially desirable as sprouted seeds is gray stripe sunflower. It is best to serve these sprouted seeds when the sprout is just starting to show through the end of the seed husk. If the sprout grows too long, the bird will cut it off and lose the benefit of the sprouting process. Many breeders also sprout a mixture of legumes and then lightly cook them and mix them with cooked brown rice for a nice warm meal on cold days or during the breeding season. Sprouting is easily accomplished by soaking overnight the required amount of seeds covered in water. The next morning the seeds are rinsed and allowed to set in a jar, pan or sprouting device. They should be rinsed later in the day also. If the weather or environment is in the seventy degrees Fahrenheit (21c) or warmer, the sunflower seeds will sprout in twenty-four hours and be ready for rinsing and adding to the daily soft food mixture. Other seeds may require a longer timeline, with some of the legumes requiring two to three days. Immediately prior to serving the sprouted seeds or beans, it is advisable to soak them in a solution of water and hydrogen peroxide for five minutes. This solution, one-quarter cup of hydrogen peroxide to half a gallon of water, works on the seed surface and removes debris, old seed skin, and cleans the surface of the seed husk and the sprouts so that you are feeding a very clean food item. After soaking, rinse well in fresh water.

Pelleted Diets. There are presently a wide variety of pelleted diets available for feeding parrots and the manufacturers have even formulated some specifically for Eclectus parrots. Eclectus parrots can benefit from the daily addition to their diet of a small amount of pellets, say about a quarter cup per bird. Pellets should not be the main portion of any Eclectus parrot diet. Indeed, an Eclectus parrot can survive quite well on a diet that does not contain any pellets at all.

Colored Pellets. Although several manufacturers have produced colored pellets specifically for Eclectus parrots, it is not recommended that Eclectus parrots be fed colored pellets at all. It appears that for many Eclectus parrots a diet of colored pellets interferes with the bird's ability to produce red feathers after a moult. This is especially true of the primarily red female Eclectus parrots. When new feathers are produced, the red feathers often contain yellow stripes or yellow areas. Sometimes this is a bright yellow and sometimes it is more of a dark dusty yellow. Apparently the colored dyes inhibit the production of red during the development of the feathers. There have been no studies to determine whether or not other types of changes in the bird's physiology have occurred due to the consumption of colored pellets. Since we do not know exactly what effect these pellets are having, besides affecting the production of the red in feathers, it is recommended that colored pellets be omitted from the diet of Eclectus parrots.

Feeding Young Eclectus Parrots. It is very important that young weaning or weaned Eclectus parrots be provided with a good variety of foods so that the young bird is exposed to these foods at an age when he or she will be interested and will accept this variety. When young birds are fed a limited diet for the many months of their early learning about foods, they may develop the habit of not eating anything with which they are unfamiliar. If you find this to be the case, one solution is to take the item you want them to accept and to eat it in front of them. Young healthy hand reared Eclectus parrots will be full of a balance of vitamins and minerals from their hand feeding formula and these birds do not respond well to additional vitamins and minerals provided on their food or in their food. It is advised that young Eclectus parrots be provided their soft foods in a wide bowl so that they can readily see all the items and do not have to toss out items to find their favorites.

Food Bowl Location. Since young birds instinctively do not want to go to the bottom of the cage or to a low perch, it is important that the food dishes be made available at the higher perches where the bird will feel comfortable in sitting and eating. Making the food bowls easily accessible is very important, as it seems to take young birds a major part of their day just to eat enough food. They are not as adept at removing seed hulls and then consuming the contents, or handling and eating their vegetables and fruits.

Eclectus Behavior. How are Eclectus parrots different from other species? One area is their activity level. Eclectus might be considered less active than the small Cockatoos, such as the Galah and less active than most Lories and other small parrots. This does not mean that Eclectus are sedentary or inactive. They are very observant about everything around them. When placed into a new situation, Eclectus parrots spend hours studying their new surroundings. After they have familiarized themselves with everything, they then proceed to go about their routine activities of eating, playing, grooming and communicating. Therefore, if you move your bird's cage from one room to another, you can expect that the Eclectus will become very quiet for several hours or even a day or two, sometimes hardly eating.

Eclectus parrots are active birds and enjoy climbing their cage and hanging upside down from the cage top, playing on a springy hanging perch or flying around the house, sometimes in search of you, sometimes from one favorite perch to another. It is recommended that you have two main locations for Eclectus activities: the cage itself and a secondary perch in some other location, such as a climbing tree with hanging toys and food cups, or an assemblage of perches and toys on a movable table or floor stand.

All play areas need access to food and water, especially for Eclectus parrots under two years of age as they are still in a developmental mode and will want to have a bite to eat during play times. The best climbing areas and perches will have a variety of perch sizes as well as different surfaces, from natural wood branches to firm woven fabric perches so that the bird has relief from perching on only one type of surface. Plastic toys are fine as long as the plastic is solid and sturdy and pieces cannot be chewed or bitten off. A combination of soft wood shapes and plastic shapes strung on a natural rawhide cord are greatly enjoyed. Eclectus also enjoy shredding paper or cardboard, which should only be provided if it is clean and not treated with chemicals or waxes. You do not want to expose the birds to any chemicals or materials such as lead or zinc. Such metals can result in illness and death if ingested by the bird. There are medical treatments, which your avian veterinarian can administer if the bird does ingest such metals.

Eclectus Frights. Some individual Eclectus, especially those of the *Eclectus roratus vosmaeri* subspecies, are occasionally extremely frightened by something very unusual, such as the sudden appearance of a small child running towards them or of an animal in their environment which they have never seen before. This can cause them to raise all their feathers and scream like banshees as they are experiencing a great fear. While in this state they may thrash about in their cage. It is best to immediately remove the offending animal or object and to talk to them to calm them down. Although most Eclectus enjoy new people and new events, there are sometimes occasions where they become extremely frightened at something very unusual.

Eclectus and Other Pets. Many families that enjoy having birds also enjoy other pet animals, most commonly dogs or cats. When there are dogs and cats in the household, there are two major concerns for your companion Eclectus parrot. 1) Physical harm or death caused by the animal biting the bird, and 2) the introduction of gram negative bacteria from the dog or cat via a bite, or scratch to the bird, or from the bird eating from the dog or cat's food dish. Birds should not be allowed outside the cage when cats and dogs are present unless you are also present. Birds should not be outside their cage in a darkened room when dogs or cats are present as predatory animal instinct takes over in dogs and cats if the bird is fluttering about in the dark room. Hunting dogs can be especially dangerous around pet birds unless they have been well trained and have learned to leave the bird alone.

Sometimes the dog or cat will become a close friend to the bird. This is not a problem unless the dog or cat licks the bird. The mouth of a dog or cat contains gram negative bacteria that are dangerous for the bird. The bacteria will remain on the feathers and the bird will ingest it as it preens its feathers. This can lead to illness in the bird. If a cat scratches a bird's skin, the bird should be immediately taken to a veterinarian as potentially fatal bacteria can be introduced from the cat's claws and teeth. Many bird owners also have cats and dogs and they all live together quite nicely. The main concern to keep in mind is that birds and other pets should be monitored when they are free in the same environment.

Visiting the Veterinarian. Sometimes it is advisable to take a companion Eclectus parrot to the veterinarian for a routine check up or for special medical diagnosis if the bird appears to be unwell. A sick Eclectus will be very quiet and not vocalizing as usual, sitting in one spot, with head tucked into the shoulder area and feathers slightly lofted or raised, in order to maintain its proper body temperature. You may also find that the feces do not appear to be normal in size, appearance or amount. If indications are such that a trip to the veterinarian is advised, you should make the appointment and place the bird into the carrier at the last minute prior to leaving the house, making the trip straight to the appointment. This is to reduce the stress on the bird, which will affect the white blood count that shows up in the blood tests. In addition, it is advisable to stay with your bird while testing and handling is done so that you are very familiar with exactly what is happening to your bird. Ask the veterinarian to explain all procedures and treatments, their purpose and possible side effects.

Sometimes pet owners ask the veterinarian to groom their bird, i.e. to trim toenails and to clip wings. It is very important that toenail clipping be done with great care and very little of the nail removed or the bird will have sore toes. This causes the bird to be unable to perch correctly and even causes it to fall off the perch, with the potential for breaking bones and receiving other injuries. It is recommended that the wings of Eclectus parrots remain intact in order to prevent the unwanted behavior of feather chewing or plucking. It is thought that severe wing trims in Eclectus, those that have the primaries clipped down to the coverts, encourages feather picking. The cut edges of the primaries dig into the sides of the bird and the bird is forever trying to groom those cut ends. The bird often develops a repetitive feather grooming behavior which can develop into feather picking behavior. If Eclectus wings must be clipped, it is recommended that the clip be a light or brief clipping of the outer 1/3 of the first primary feathers, starting at the outside edge of the wing, and ending up making the cut even with the secondary feathers. This allows the bird a certain amount of flying ability and greatly reduces the possibility of feather picking.

Keeping Your Eclectus Parrot Happy. It should be relatively easy to maintain a continuous happy relationship with your Eclectus parrot. Following are some simple guidelines that should make that happen. Be sure to provide a daily diet of a variety of fresh vegetables and fruits, greens and sprouted seeds, along with fresh water. Make it a routine to clean the perches and cage sides each week, as well as the cage bottom. Talk to your Eclectus parrot before you expect to pick up the bird or handle it. Move slowly with a new bird or a young bird as fast movement is threatening. Provide as large a cage as possible, but certainly at least three feet in width and two feet in depth for one Eclectus parrot. Purchase a variety of soft wood toys and rotate them on a weekly basis so that the bird has several toys to enjoy each week but cannot become bored with exactly the same toy month after month. Provide a swing or similar object that the bird can use as a swing. Give the bird a shower or bath at least three times a week. Make sure that grooming of the toenails and the wings is not excessive so that the bird is able to maintain its balance and perching ability and is not encouraged to chew on its wing feathers. Provide at least one perch in a soft chewable wood so that the Eclectus parrot can keep its beak groomed by chewing on that perch. Set in place a relationship with a veterinarian so that you have one available when you have need for one. Do not try to force your bird to be something you want that the bird is not designed to be. Do not expect your bird to be like a cockatoo, or a dog or cat. Keep your expectations realistic. Remember to enjoy your bird every day. If you follow these basic guidelines, you should have an affectionate, talkative, beautiful and healthy companion Eclectus parrot.

Chapter 8
The Importance of Keeping Records

Every bird kept should have its own personal record file. This can be either a card record keeping system that is simple and kept on hand in the bird room, or a more detailed record kept on your computer. I recommend both systems because when you are busy working outdoors and you want to access a file quickly then it's on hand where you work.

Each file should contain the bird's identification number or leg band number including the aviary number where the bird was housed. The bird's parents' identification numbers and any relevant information such as date of birth and age, any previous medical history should be recorded, notes on medication, dose rate and length of the treatment listed. When a mature bird becomes ill then its medical history may show that it has had this problem in the past and will show how it was treated. These are all relevant facts to maintaining a healthy breeding collection.

By writing the information down, whether on a card file or computer, is far better than trying to commit the information to memory. When I first started keeping birds I relied on my memory for the information, but soon realized that with the number of birds that I was keeping at the time it soon would become a problem trying to remember everything. I started carrying a note book with me at all times and would jot down information as I fed out each day, then it would rain and my notes would get wet and the information would at the best of times be hard to read. So I started a card file and then upgraded to a computer, now all my files are at least readable.

During my time as bird curator/manager at the Pearl Coast Zoological Gardens Broome, Western Australia, we had in place an excellent system for the keeping of records. This system my son and I continued when we started the Avicultural Breeding and Research Centre at Bonville, New South Wales in 1993. Here we were specializing in the sub species of Eclectus parrots that were available at the time in Australia.

These records consisted of five main reports and these are:

1. Nestcheck Report.
2. Young Breakdown Report.
3. Specimen Report.
4. Taxon Report.
5. Sales Report.

The nestcheck report as its name suggests is for keeping a record of the nesting information during regular nest inspections. At the zoo in Broome our bird keepers conducted weekly nest inspections. Because the zoo housed over 1500 birds in over 300 aviaries the bird department was divided into sections. Each section had two regular keepers assigned to it for at least a three-month period. These keepers worked to a roster and were responsible for the daily upkeep of the birds and aviaries in that section, this also involved the weekly nestcheck. Each bird keeper would conduct the weekly nestcheck accompanied by the bird curator and inspected every nest in their section. Each aviary and every pair housed in that aviary were checked and nesting activity recorded. If any eggs or chicks were counted then these details were recorded on their nestcheck sheet.

The nestcheck record sheet listed the species, the aviary number in which it was housed, the male and female identification numbers and the two previous nest check details stating the number of eggs or chicks or nest activity of that particular aviary. If there were multiple pairs and nesting sites then the nest box number was added to the nestcheck report. After the weekly nestcheck was completed a copy was given to the records officer and added to the computer records. The original copy was retained by the bird keeper and filed in the bird room.

Keeping detailed records of nesting activity and nest contents during the breeding season will be of great benefit when it comes time to leg band the chicks and to predict when they are due to fledge. This will allow the bird keeper to be more observant at this time so any newly fledged chicks are not startled when they enter the aviary, which may cause them to fly into the wire and injure themselves.

Having weekly nest checks and recording the information will also be helpful in keeping track of a particular pair of birds' breeding history. If this pair has a history of infertile eggs and after a period of time continues to do so, then the bird keeper can be told to observe this pair to see if they are compatible, see if he is feeding the female, and activity such as mating observed. If there is no compatibility then the pair could be moved to another aviary or the pair broken up and re-paired.

Young breakdown record sheet. When fledglings are removed for hand feeding or leave the nest they are added to the young breakdown record sheet. This record sheet keeps track of all the young produced and their availability for future breeding or sale. The young breakdown record sheet contains such information as their identification number (computer number), date it was removed from the nest or fledged, sex, species or sub species, aviary number where it came from, the parents' identification numbers, its own leg band number and the new aviary or holding cage number where it will be housed.

The young breakdown record sheet is kept available in the bird room, and is referred to when orders are received from perspective buyers inquiring about the availability of birds for sale. At a glance all the relevant details are available, such as age and sex of the bird and when it will be old enough for shipping etc. Also if the purchaser wants an unrelated pair about the same age it's just a matter of checking down the same list to see if there is a suitable match, as all the relevant details are there.

This young breakdown record sheet was of great benefit to my son and me when we were building up the numbers of Australian Eclectus parrots *Eclectus roratus macgillivrayi*. The numbers of this sub species have always been low in captivity here in Australia and as none were recorded overseas, we knew it was extremely important to maintain pure bloodlines for this sub species if we were going to be successful in developing a captive-breeding program for them. So maintaining good records of every bird in our collection made this process an easy one.

All young produced were added to this report and as I was responsible for the hand feeding of most of the young produced at our facility I was in the best position to notice any extra qualities within a particular bird. If a particular bird showed signs of being of robust quality or was slightly larger or had a wider head I would note these remarks on the young breakdown report sheet. And by the time the bird had fledged I would have decided whether to retain this bird for future breeding or offer it for sale.

Of course as it happens in most cases your best young come from one or two of your best breeding pairs, and it would be impossible to keep them all. Some of these extra special young birds were kept up to two or three years hoping we would be able to produce a suitable unrelated mate for them, and in many cases we managed to do just this, but a few had to be sold.

The specimen report. When a bird was sold the purchaser was offered a specimen report. The specimen report is like an official receipt but contained a lot more information on the bird and its genetic history. If a bird was paid for and was being shipped to the purchaser then the specimen report was attached with the other documents on the shipping box.

The specimen report contained the species and sub species name as well as the common name of the bird. It listed its computer number, its date of birth, its date of removal from the nest, its age at the date of sale, its sex and house name, its leg band number and aviary number of where it was bred and also the aviary or holding cage where it recently was housed. This specimen report also contained its parents' identification numbers and its hand feeding history as well as the purchaser's name and phone number. All relevant information the purchaser required about the bird and its genetic history was made available. If the purchaser retains their copy of the specimen report it becomes extremely important to them when they decide to purchase another Eclectus parrot from us as they would be able to verify that their new purchase was an unrelated bird to the one they purchased previously.

It has even been possible at a much later date in matching up single birds purchased from us with young birds produced since that original sale, but only by keeping these type of reports. All breeders should be encouraged to keep proper and accurate records and to offer to their prospective buyers this information.

The taxon report is an in-house computer report that records all the birds of a particular species or sub species, for example our Red-sided or New Guinea Eclectus parrots *Eclectus roratus polychloros.* All birds including adults, breeding birds and young birds are recorded here, starting with our older birds and breeders, and then moving down to the latest youngsters.

When a chick is recorded on its first nest check report it is then added to the taxon report. It is given a computer number which is also its taxon number. When young Eclectus parrot chicks have broken color they are sexed and leg banded with a seven digit code i.e. A.B.R.C.

187. This leg band number and the bird's sex is added to the taxon report.

The taxon report is in a spreadsheet format on the computer and contains information such as the taxon name (species name), common name i.e. Red sided Eclectus parrot. Each bird listed starts off with its taxon number (computer number) then its leg band number with either the letters R/L or L/L after it, this indicates which leg the leg band is attached too (right leg for males and left leg for females). The aviary number where the bird is housed is also recorded as well as the bird's date of birth. Each time a taxon report is printed out it will give the exact age of each bird to the day i.e.1year 4months and 5days. This type of report is very helpful when pairing up juvenile birds as future breeding pairs. At the start of each breeding season we would sit down and review this list and pair up birds that were of suitable ages for breeding.

The taxon report also contained information on when a particular bird came into our facility. If we bred the bird then its birth date would be shown in the "in" section and if the bird were sold the date of the sale would be shown in the "out" section. The next section listed if the bird was wild born or captive born, and if the bird was purchased or bred by us. If the bird was bred by us then the sire and dam's (parents, identification) numbers would be listed as well.

When the taxon report is printed out a summary of all birds held is listed at the end of the report, plus the report end date. Totals held: i.e. 11.8.1 (11males + 8 females + 1unsexed =20 animals), 20 animal's captive born, 0 wild born. The acquisition summary: 8.5.1 by birth =14, plus 3.3.0 purchased from elsewhere. Therefore the total numbers of New Guinea Eclectus *Eclectus roratus polychloros* held by us at the date of this report was 11 males, 8 females and one unsexed chick, a total of 20 animals.

The taxon report when printed out at the end of the year will also show how our breeding pairs have produced that year. By simply counting down the list the number of chicks produced including the ratio of male to females can be counted by either following the aviary number or the parents' identification numbers.

The sales report is the fifth and final report. The sales report can either be kept on the computer or hand written in a ledger book. I prefer the hand written method because it is kept out in the birdroom where most sales are conducted. Listed in the sales report starting with the date of sale, then who the sale is made to. Their name and address and contact number, their aviary registration number (if required), the details of the bird or birds sold, i.e. sex, taxon number, leg band number, age, and finally the sales price, including if a deposit was paid etc.

All of the above reports are important for the smooth running of a successful breeding facility. Whether you keep five pairs or a hundred pairs the keeping of accurate records is a must.

Bibliography

Arthur K, Bauer F, and Desborough L. (1987) *A Complete Guide to Eclectus Parrots*. Parrot Publishing Company, San Francisco, U.S.A.

Austin C. (1956). *Range extension of three bird species*. Emu, Vol.56 pp.80-81.

Bowler J. and Taylor J. (1989) *An annotated checklist of the birds of Manusela National Park,* Seram. Kukila 4:3-29. Ornithological Society of Indonesia.

Butchart S, Brooks T, Davies C, Gunawan D. Lowen J, and Alo Sahu. (1996) *The conservation status of forest birds on Flores and Sumbawa, Indonesia.* Bird Conservation International 6:335-370.

Catterall M. (1998) *The parrots of Buton Island, South West Sulawesi.* PsittaScene 10(2): 10-11.

Charpentier S, and Guerquin F. (1997) *Ambon/Seram.* BirdLife International. Bogor, Indonesia.

Cayley N. (1959) *What Bird is That.* Angus and Robertson, Sydney.

Draffan, R. D.W., Garnett, S. T. and Malone, G. J. 1983. Bird of the Torres Strait: An annotated list and biogeographic analysis. *Emu 83:207-234.*

Desborough L. (2001) *Some notes on the Biaki Eclectus parrot Eclectus roratus biaki.* Personal correspondence.

Forshaw J. (1973) *Parrots of the World.* Lansdowne Press, Melbourne.

Forshaw J. (1969) *Australian Parrots.* Lansdowne Press, Melbourne.

Fuller R. (undated) *Avifaunal survey, Halmahera 1994, University of Bristol Expedition to Indonesia.* BirdLife International, Cambridge.

Grey G. (1861) *List of birds collected by Wallace at the Maluku Islands.* Proc. Zool. Soc. London: 341-366.

Guillemard F. (1855a) *Report on the collections of birds from the island of Sumbawa, Indonesia.* Proc. Zool. Soc. London: 501-511.

Guillemard F. (1855b) *Report on the collection of birds from Celebes.* Proc. Zool. Soc. London: 542-561.

Guillemard F. (1855c) *Report on the collection of birds from the Molucca Islands.* Proc. Zool. Soc. London: 561-576.

Hartert E. (1898) *Account of the birds collected on the island of Sumba by Alfred Everett and native collectors.* Novit. Zool. 5: 466-476.

Hartert E. (1900) *The birds of Dammer Island in the Banda Sea.* Novit. Zool. 7: 12-24.

Holmes D. (1993a) *Birds on Sumba: a synopsis of birds recorded on the island of Sumba 1991.* BirdLife International, Cambridge.

Holmes D. (1993b) *Birds on Timor: a synopsis of birds recorded on Timor, 1993.* BirdLife International, Cambridge.

Holmes D. (1993c) *Birds on Flores: a synopsis of birds recorded on the island of Flores, 1993.* BirdLife International, Cambridge.

Hornskov J. (1992) *Observations of birds by G. Speight and J. Hornskov on the islands of Sulawesi, Halmahera and Timor in 1991.* © Jesper Hornskov 1992.

Iredale T. (1956) *Birds of New Guinea.* Georgian House, Melbourne.

Johnstone R, Van Balen S, and Dekker R. (1993) *New bird records for the island of Lombok.* Kukila 6: 124-127.

Jones M, Linsley M, and Marsden S. (1995) *Population sizes, status and habitat associations of the restricted-range bird species of Sumba, Indonesia.* Bird Conservation International, 5: 21-52.

Jones M, and Marsden S. (undated) *Conservation of key forests and their threatened birds on Sumba.* Bird Conservation International, Draft Report.

Kendall S. (1979) *Citron-crested Cockatoos in Sumba.* Avicultural Mag. 8: 93-94.

Lambert F. (1994) *Notes on the avifauna of Bacan, Kasiruta and Obi, North Moluccas.* Kukila 7: 1-9.

Lambert F. (1993) *The status and trade of North Malukan parrots with particular emphasis on Cacatua alba, Lorius garrulus and Eos squamata.* Gland, Switzerland: IUCN-The World Conservation Union.

Lambert F, and Yong D. (1989) *Some recent bird observations from Halmahera.* Kukila 4: 30-33.

Lendon A. (1946) *Memories of the Moluccas.* Aviculture Mag. 52:206-213.

Low R. (1980) *Parrots their Care and Breeding.* Blandford Press Ltd. Dorset.

Marsden S. and Jones M. (1997) *The nesting requirements of the parrots and hornbill of Sumba, Indonesia.* Biological Conservation, 82: 279-287.

Marsden S, Jones M, Linsley M, Mead C, and Hounsome M. (1997) *The conservation status of the restricted-range lowland birds of Buru, Indonesia.* Bird Conservation International, 7:213-233.

Mayr E. (1944) *The birds of Timor and Sumba.* American Museum of Natural History, 83:123-194.

Poulsen M, and Jepson P. (1996) *Status of the Salmon-crested Cockatoo and Red Lory on Ambon Island, Maluku.* Kukila 8:159-160.

Sclater P. (1883) *Birds collected on Timor-Laut or Tanimbar group of islands by Henry O. Forbes.* Proc. Zool. Soc. London: 48-58.

Sotheby's (1998) *Biblotheque Marcel Jeanson Deuxieme Partie Ornithologie, Monaco.* Sotheby's Monaco.

Sweeney R. (1993) *The Eclectus A Complete Guide.* Silvio Mattacchione and Co. Ontario.

Smiet F. (1985) *Notes on the field status and trade of Moluccan parrots.* Biological Conservation, 34: 181-194.

Stresemann E. (1934) *Uber Vogel, gesammelt von Dr F. Kopstein auf den Sud-Molukken und Tanimbar1922-1924.* Zool. Meded. 17: 15-19.

Verbelen F. (1994) *Birding in Seram, Kai, and Tanimbar, Indonesia.* BirdLife International, Cambridge.

Verheijen J (1961) *some notes on the birds of the island of Palue, flores, Indonesia.* Ardea 49: 183-186.

White C, and Bruce M. (1986) *The birds of Wallacea (Sulawesi, the Moluccas and Lesser Sunda Islands, Indonesia).* British Ornithologists' Union, London.